LEADERSHIP IN THE CHURCH
FOR A PEOPLE OF HOPE

LEADERSHIP IN THE CHURCH
FOR A PEOPLE OF HOPE

Mervyn Davies
and
Graham Dodds

t&t clark

Published by T&T Clark International
A Continuum Imprint
The Tower Building, 11 York Road, London SE1 7NX
80 Maiden Lane, Suite 704, New York, NY 10038

www.continuumbooks.com

British Library Cataloguing-in-Publication Data
A catalogue record for this book is available from the British Library

ISBN: 978-0-567-38621-2 (hardback)
       978-0-567-01407-8 (paperback)

Typeset by Fakenham Prepress Solutions, Fakenham, Norfolk NR21 8NN
Printed and bound in Great Britain

TABLE OF CONTENTS

FOREWORD

There have been many books written on leadership in an age when the leaders of organizations are more and more under scrutiny in the world's media. It matters now, more than ever before, what decisions are made by leaders in other countries, in multinational corporations, in sport, banking, the Health Service, Social Services, education, politics and in the Church. Painfully, perhaps, the churches have had to adopt more and more of the professional practices and procedures for accountability, originating in the secular sphere, particularly when failures in good practice have been mercilessly and rightly exposed. Church members in secular organizations often express frustration at the lack of good management practice in the church and want to do something about it. This is sometimes resisted, as theological language becomes increasingly replaced by secular terms and the churches respond by setting up professional practices and standards. These may seem at variance with the more traditional understanding of the ordained role as a *vocation* rather than as contracted employment with a job description and conditions of service containing a raft of obligations and bench marks. Is there a danger of something being lost here?

The privatization of religion that is being experienced in society today appears to ensure that it is difficult to make any overt claim to be a *Christian* leader in business but especially in politics. Is discipleship to be exercised only in secret and in our spare time? Within the churches themselves, the decline in membership together with a greater emphasis on paid as well as voluntary lay participation in ministry, has arguably led to uncertainty about what the ordained role is anyway, as well as raising issues about how the laity can exercise leadership within and outside the Church or how their gifts and time are to be used and managed.

This book seeks to bring together these two languages of organizational theory on the one hand, and theology and spirituality on the other, and to link them to ecclesiology, that is, the Church's understanding of itself. It is therefore largely a work of theology drawing in particular on the pioneering writings of writers like Newman, Congar, Zizioulas, Dulles and others who have contributed so much to our understanding of the Church. We believe that while it is right to insist on good institutional practices, the Church and its ministry are not simply to be understood in management terms. The solution to some of the difficulties that have been experienced in the past are not likely to be solved simply by the imposition of secular models of contemporary organizational practice which may need, in any case, to be critiqued. These must be brought alongside the Christian images, metaphors, narratives and symbols which need to be explored and reflected on empathetically, for that is how much of the Christian self-understanding has necessarily been expressed. It is equally true that because of the Church's prophetical calling, society has something to gain from Christian theology and faith perspectives even though it also needs its own language from which the Church can learn. This also requires a link to be made with mission, for the Church needs to be visibly *within* society, in dialogue and debate with it and this, too, requires leadership and a right understanding of both the lay and the ordained roles and vocations.

Leadership in the Church for a People of Hope is intended not so much as a practical manual in leadership (although some suggestions for this are included) but as a theological exploration which tries to clarify some of the confusion about the Church and its ministry. It is an ecumenical study bringing together insights from different parts of the Christian Church and their traditions and as such is an example of what has been called Receptive Ecumenism in which denominations of the Church learn from each other rather than emphasizing differences and problems. As such, therefore, the book is aimed at those in training for the ordained ministry as well as clergy already in post, laity involved with work for or on behalf of the Church, Christians in secular employment and the interested and concerned reader who wishes to explore a practical ecclesiology that tries to unravel some important theological issues and problems.

Most of the material for this book had its origins over a period of many years in conferences, training workshops and seminars principally in the Diocese of Bath & Wells but also in the Dioceses of Exeter, Rochester, Salisbury, the RC Diocese of Clifton as well as at Wesley College, Bristol, Oscott College Seminary in Birmingham, the West of England Ministerial Training Course, and the Bristol Methodist District. Some material had its origins in management training courses for senior staff in the former County of Avon.

Elements from all these courses led to a module, validated by the University of the West of England and later by the University of Bristol, entitled *Leadership in the Church* at Wesley College for ministers and pastors who wished to examine and reflect on their experiences as leaders. This involved ten units, sometimes spread over five one-day events and others over ten weeks. The sessions included ecclesiology, consideration of foundational roles, the nature of authority for leadership, servant leadership, leadership of change, collaborative ministry, how to handle conflict using insights from Transactional Analysis, managing volunteers, the spirituality of time and how to be a learning community. These themes and much more have been developed further here.

This course was adapted and extended to be used in the Diocese of Bath & Wells for clergy in post and newly appointed clergy in virtually all parishes, an initiative first pioneered by Revd Canon Russell Bowman-Eadie, Director of Training and delivered always by a team of which he was always an inspiration as well as a collaborative colleague. Insights were also used from previous diocesan initiatives such as a church that wanted a Lent course. *Easter People* was devised as a pilot by the minister, Revd Mike Slade and several course designers including Steve Annandale, Revd Jennifer Cole and Phil Kirk, former principal lecturer in Organisation Studies in the University of the West of England Business School, who has researched extensively in the area of secular leadership and had already developed a model of leadership known as *See, Walk, Talk.* His work outlined in *Local Ministry Story, Process and Meaning,* offers opportunities for churches to exercise connective leadership, empowerment and dialogue to 'create vision, mobilize energy and inspire action'.

In the preparation of this book, the authors wish to acknowledge the valuable help and advice from the many colleagues, some of whom are mentioned above, with whom we have worked. As facilitators of leadership courses, our experience has also been of a two-way learning process and so our thanks go to all those who participated for their insights and wisdom from which we have benefited but who, of course, bear no responsibility for any shortcomings in these pages.

Our particularly warm thanks go to Revd Jennifer Cole whose diligent preparation, editing and proofreading of the manuscript of this book, has been invaluable and who made important and helpful suggestions that improved it. Any remaining shortcomings are, of course, the responsibility of the authors.

Chapter 1

CHURCH AND SOCIETY: THE STATE WE'RE IN

In 1996 a very readable and controversial book about the British economy was re-published in paperback form entitled *The State We're In* by Will Hutton, then editor of *The Observer*.[1] In it, Hutton sought to give an analysis of the state of the economy and argued that British society was fracturing, investment was too low and that our democratic systems were suffering from structural deformations that have profoundly negative effects on decision making. He tried to show how deep-seated in British history and culture these problems are and that therefore this makes them all the more difficult to eradicate. He argued forcefully against the view that the UK had little to learn from other parts of the world, challenged some of the accepted wisdom about capitalism, e.g. that it is only successful on the basis of individualistic and competitive strategies rather than collaboration and consensus, and tried to set out what he considered were the principles upon which true wealth creation can take place. We need, he suggested, thinking in the long term, engaging in the right kind of investment, and having appropriate and dynamic forms of decision making and proper accountability. Britain, he argued, suffers from short-termism and ways of thinking that seem to imply that our institutions are in no need of change and somehow set in concrete. He maintained that we need to move to what he calls 'relational capitalism'.[2]

Events towards the end of the first decade of the new millennium seemed to prove him right, as the major world economies in 2008–09 went into one of the severest recessions for many years, which was widely blamed on recklessness and greed in the financial sector and,

[1]   Hutton, W. (1996) *The State We're In* (new and revised edition). London: Vintage.
[2]   Ibid. Preface.

1

even more importantly, to the loss of any real sense of morality in the market economy. This was followed by revelations in 2009 about the abuse of the payment for expenses system by MPs that led to a sense of moral outrage that rocked the nation. Then there were allegations of phone tapping and of dubious practices by the press. The search for people and institutions to blame for the ills of society seems to show no sign of ending. These events led Lord Sacks, Chief Rabbi of the United Hebrew Congregations of the Commonwealth to ask:

> The big question is: how do we learn to be moral again? Markets were made to serve us; we were not made to serve markets. Economics needs ethics. Markets do not survive by market forces alone. They depend on respect for the people affected by our decisions. Lose that and we lose not just money but something more significant still: freedom, trust and decency, the things that have a value, not a price.[3]

Inevitably, Hutton's book aroused a good deal of debate because it challenged a number of cherished assumptions as he tried to discern what the underlying trends may be and to find positive ways forward. Events since have made this challenge all the more urgent, as critics sought to analyze the causes of a financial failure that may have consequences for our society for decades to come and which can now be seen, by hindsight, to be but symptoms of a more widespread malaise. What may be hopeful about this is a growing recognition that this raises questions about public and private morality, responsibility and leadership as well as human error. The Church, of course, is part of this context and affected by it as it considers its future. If, through its members and as an institution, it has to recognize that it is part of the problem, it needs to consider how it may contribute to the solution and form leaders who can help this to happen.

Lord Sacks had reflected on this in his address to the 2008 Lambeth Conference in calling for a renewal of the sense of covenant by which he meant, among other things, bonds of reciprocity, trust and cooperation, a bedrock found in religion:

> What then happens to a society when religion wanes and there is nothing covenantal to take its place? Relationships break down. Marriages grow weak. Families become fragile. Communities atrophy. And the result is that people feel vulnerable and alone. If they turn these feelings outward, the result is often anger turning to violence. If they turn them inward, the result is depression, stress related syndromes, eating disorders and drug and alcohol abuse. Either way there is spiritual poverty in the midst of material affluence. It doesn't

---

[3] Sacks, Jonathan, 'Morals: the one thing markets don't make', Opinion *The Times*, Saturday 21 March 2009.

happen all at once, but slowly, gradually and inexorably. Societies, without covenants and the institutions needed to sustain them, disintegrate.[4]

AREAS OF CONCERN

In 1985, the Church of England published its searching report on Urban Priority Areas *Faith in the City – A Call for Action by Church and Nation*[5] which called attention to a pervasive situation of poverty and powerlessness in Britain's cities, which challenged both Church and government to have faith in our cities to remedy endemic problems that had already been identified in the 1960s. While much has been achieved since then, the conclusion that in any analysis of our society deep questions will arise about the nature and purpose of the Church and the meaning of the Christian Gospel[6] remains as true today as it did then.

Education dominated much of the political discussions of the late twentieth century and well into the first decade of the twenty-first. The government of the day became increasingly prescriptive about what should be taught and how. Discussion of the philosophy of education virtually ceased in all PGCE (post graduate certificate in education) courses and there was little reflection also by the churches as to the theological basis for education. In higher education, theology and religious studies departments were increasingly under pressure with some closing. This was significant for church-based education at all levels, which seemed confused not only about *what the difference that makes the difference is*, but what kind of moral and spiritual leadership was needed in these institutions. The Church itself seemed to make little impact on educational thinking at national level either. If it is religion that gives meaning to the whole of life, has the Church been too timid in contributing to national discussions about the way in which lives are to be shaped in the future?

The Children's Society's *A Good Childhood: Searching for Values in a Competitive Age*[7] repays careful thought by Church leaders. While

---

[4] Lord Sacks' Address to the 2008 Lambeth Conference, 28 July 2008 http://www.bc.edu/research/cjl/meta-elements/texts/cjrelations/news/Sacks_Lambeth_Address.htm

[5] General Synod of the Church of England (1985) *Faith in the City – A Call for Action by Church and Nation*. London: Church House Publishing.

[6] *Faith in the City* (1985) p. 372.

[7] The Children's Society (2009) *A Good Childhood: Searching for Values in a Competitive Age*. London: Penguin.

there is much to celebrate in today's achievements of children, it says, there is also considerable cause for unease. Changes in work patterns, in parenting, the social and political landscape, outside influences on the lives of children, examination and testing pressures and a widening poverty gap are some of the many causes of concern as we learn that young people appear to be more anxious and troubled than in the past. How much of this is due to a dysfunctional society, to confusion about values and to a weaker sense of moral values and of community? How much of this is due to what many commentators are now arguing is an unhealthy obsession with the individual and his/her achievement at the expense of any concept of society or of belonging to it? The evidence gathered seems to support the connection.

If reflection is needed to be done about how we view society, the economy and public life, there is surely a need to do a similar exercise about the Church which is, arguably, facing one of the most significant crises in its two thousand-year history. To do so is to raise profound issues not just about how and where to direct its energies or manage ever scarcer resources, but about its own self-understanding as an institution within society. Has the Church allowed itself to be marginalized, failing in its prophetic role, thus contributing to the moral vacuum in public life highlighted by the Chief Rabbi? For Christians, the state we are in is a *theological* question, not just a *functional* one. It raises issues of leadership and success may need to be judged by a range of criteria, some of which may seem strange to a secular organization, although others may well be similar also.

How are we to describe the state we are in? How far is the Church the victim of pressures and tensions over which it has little control? Can it be said that the Church has been the architect of many of its problems through failures in leadership? In what sense can the hand of God be discerned in all this? What ways forward are open to the Church and how might these be turned into realizable strategies? These are but a few of the questions that might be asked. In the history of Israel, God seemed to allow people to be visited with calamity or disaster when they failed to live according to the Covenant, but how far is that a helpful interpretation? Isn't it always true that the *People of God* is not faithful enough, so how far does that illuminate the understanding of the situation now? Is it better to say that what is happening is some kind of indication of the movement of the Spirit in which God is saying 'I want it done differently'?

There is a danger in going exclusively for such explanations without appreciating the many other variables that need to be taken into account and therefore it can lead to responding in ways that simply ignore the context in which we live or facts that we find uncomfortable. The other variables will include sociological, political, historical and cultural changes in our society. It needs to be remembered, too, that such exclusively scriptural interpretations of events have, in the past, led to the justification of many dubious enterprises done in the name of God in which success can be seen as a sign of God's favour. Nevertheless it remains central to the Christian understanding of things that Jesus promised that the Spirit of truth would be with his followers to guide them.[8] It is therefore not a question of preferring one way of understanding the situation to all the others, but keeping a *range* of interpretations in proper tension with each other.

MODERNITY, POSTMODERNITY AND THE AUGUSTINIAN OPTION

Much has been written about the impact of modernity and postmodernity on society and, by extension on Christianity itself, in its various forms. These terms are not precise but what is clear is that challenges to the Church's position and to clerical control from alternative sources of knowledge; the social changes consequent upon the Industrial Revolution including the shift from villages to towns; alternative accounts of what it is to be human from the social sciences; the rise of democratic institutions as well as increasing individualism, have all challenged the position of the Church and many of the assumptions under which it operated. Arguably these and many other changes that have accelerated over the past two hundred years or so, have sapped the feeling of confidence that the Church once had. It raises in an acute form the question as to how the Church should relate to the world around it, when it is rapidly losing control of the agenda.

The Second Vatican Council thought it had the answer to this question, recognizing as it did, that the Church needed dialogue with the contemporary world. The Pastoral Constitution on *The Church in the Modern World,* known as *Gaudium et Spes* spoke of the role of the Church as a kind of *leaven* or *soul* of society bringing about change from within and went on confidently to describe all the ways in which it saw the potential for a mutual relationship with the society in

---

[8] Jn 16.13.

which the Church was.[9] This was warmly welcomed and a real change from the fortress model of Church that had preceded the Council. Experience, perhaps must now make us temper that optimism and evaluate how much this can really be said to be a reality in twenty-first-century Europe, which has seen a marked decline in churchgoing that can be traced back at least to the 1960s, going hand in hand with increased affluence, disengagement from traditional organizations including trade unionism but especially visible in the growth of the more transient house church and charismatic movements.

Much of traditional Christianity now seems to be typified by polarities: a loss of confidence in denominational structures but the growth of small groups or very individual forms of spirituality, ecclesially unconnected; the confidently optimistic view of the world of much post 1960s liberal theology contrasted with the emphasis on sinfulness and pessimism about humanity of the more conservative Evangelicals; the open and more relaxed style of worship that came out of the Second Vatican Council is opposed by the traditionalists who would see a return to Tridentine liturgy as vital to the renewal of the Church, are examples. If there is disagreement about the nature of the problem, there is certainly no agreement as to its resolution.

Adrian Hastings in his seminal work *A History of English Christianity 1920–1990* sums it up:

> Seen in retrospect the 1950s seem almost like a golden age of King Solomon, the sixties an era of moral prophecy of a fairly Pelagian sort. The period in which we have arrived is quite other, an age of apocalyptic, of doom watch, in which the tragedies of an anguished world become just too many to cope with, yet in which there is the strongest feeling that there may still be worse to come.[10]

Hastings goes on to argue that there are three possible responses to this view. The first is to simply despair of the kingdom and of any ultimate meaning in the world or in history and argues that many Christians in the 1980s in effect adopted this position. The second is retreat into a privately religious, sacral sphere, abandoning the struggle for the secular state as irremediably corrupt and this, too, he says has been seen to be attractive by many Christians. The last position, he says, is that of Augustine in *The City of God*, which is to take the long view of a Christian belief in the ultimate redeemability

---

[9] Abbott, W. (1966) (ed.) *The Documents of Vatican II*. London: Chapman.
[10] Hastings, A. (1991) *A History of English Christianity 1920–1990* (3rd edn). London: SCM/Philadelphia: Trinity Press International.

of things, despite all apparent evidence to the contrary. Rather fewer, he suggests, seem to want to adopt this view.[11] What sort of leadership is required for this?

If the first position is to throw in the towel, the second is an attempt to live by two moralities; one private (religious) the other public (secular), the third position is to elect to be in the world but not of it, which is the most difficult of all to occupy, requiring the Church to be a people of hope and subject to tension.

This might seem an overly pessimistic perspective with not enough emphasis on the many oases of Christian vitality that can be found, but we have to remember that the twentieth century in particular must rank as the most violent and destructive in human history and the twenty-first century, with its phenomenon of ideological terrorism, seems to be continuing the trend, although many positive things can and should be said in favour of what has been achieved. We should also have a sense of history; it seems often to be the case that when the situation of the Church seems most critical, new life and vitality comes, but not without some prophetic discernment of what our response should be to initiatives that may not be from ourselves.

SECULARISM AND THE NEW ATHEISM

If Hastings is right, then it may be that what the Church has to do is not just take the long view, but try to view its situation more as an opportunity to recover its Gospel role than an insuperable problem from which it must try and recover as best it can. At first, the grounds for optimism may not seem good, as we face what appears to be the inexorable march of secularism. Wilson in his important work *Religion in Sociological Perspective*[12] provides us with a useful definition of this phenomenon, which can be summarized as follows:

- The sequestration by political powers of the property and facilities of religious agencies.
- The shift from religious to secular control; of the various activities and functions of religion.
- The decline in the proportion of time, resources and energy given to religion.

[11] Hastings (1991) p. 660.
[12] Wilson, B. R. (1982) *Religion in Sociological Perspective.* Oxford: Oxford University Press.

- The decay of religious institutions.
- The supplanting of religious precepts by demands that accord with strictly technical criteria.
- The gradual replacement of a specifically religious consciousness by an empirical rational and instrumental orientation.
- The abandonment of mythical, poetic and artistic interpretations of nature and society in favour of matter-of-fact description.[13]

All this leads to a privatization of values and beliefs. Another way of describing this is provided by Steve Bruce[14] who sees it manifested in a decline of the importance of religion in such areas as the state and the economy, the fall in the social standing of religious roles and institutions and a decline in the extent to which people engage in religious practice. Some would argue that this has left a void, which the secular state now has to fill with such secondary school courses as Citizenship, and Personal and Social Education with part of the debate being fuelled in Britain about what can be meant by British identity and values in what is now a multicultural and multi-ethnic society. This in turn has sparked questions about the ways in which multiculturalism has been implemented and, for the churches, how to conduct interfaith dialogue and what this might mean for traditional Christian beliefs. Secularization has, arguably, created a vacuum which will simply be filled by other forms of ideology.

Charles Taylor's analysis in *A Secular Age* is similar to this in that he distinguishes between three senses of secularism: the first is the emptying of God from public spaces or of any reference to ultimate reality, so that we function within our various forms of human activity without any reference to God; the second is the falling off of religious practice and decline in churchgoing; the third is what he calls the conditions of belief in which religious belief is simply *one* option among others and the emergence of milieux in which faith may be very difficult even for the staunchest believer. In other words, the former context of understanding in which faith was axiomatic has radically changed and perhaps has gone for the foreseeable future.[15]

The scathing attack by Richard Dawkins and others on the irrationality of religion in a series of books he has published since 1976 culminating in *The God Delusion* in 2006 was symptomatic of the position in which the Church finds itself. There Dawkins describes

[13] Wilson (1982) p. 149.

[14] Bruce, S. (2002) *God is Dead, Secularization in the West.* Oxford: Blackwell, p. 3.

[15] Taylor, C. (2007) *A Secular Age.* Cambridge Mass: Belknap Press, pp. 57.

God as a 'psychotic infant' invented by mad, deluded people and faith as a form of 'blind trust, in the absence of evidence'.[16] New Atheism does not simply attack the intellectual credentials of theism, it claims religion is damaging to both society and to persons. Religions are the enemy of human and aesthetic values. There is nothing new in this – but what is new is the passion with which religion is attacked and the lack of measure in the attack. By contrast, there is a striking optimism about the prospects for human life without religion. The source of human evil is externalized and located in religion or is mocked rather than seriously engaged with, and is increasingly given *no quarter* in the public square.

Several commentators have described this New Atheism as a form of fundamentalism. Fundamentalism is the tendency to conflate and to reduce all expression of truth into a form of literalism and in consequence to attribute to a particular discipline more than is warranted or intended, resulting in a kind of caricature. It knows only one kind of truth. If we now have secular forms of fundamentalism in the shape of Dawkins and others who radically misrepresent religious belief, we must remember, too that Christians have produced their own varieties, resulting in a needless hostility and misunderstanding of science and religion that may coincide with and fuel popular prejudices against belief. The fact that terrorism has been associated with some sections of the Muslim community has not helped this either, despite the fact the vast majority of Muslims have distanced themselves from the atrocities perpetrated in their name. But, as Beattie has pointed out, the problem is wider than that and we need to consider how ideas and beliefs function within society and resist the impoverishment of religious discourse even by it adherents.[17] The multi-ethnic society, which is Britain in the twenty-first century, will require leaders in the Church who understand and can reach out to those of other faiths, promoting a similar spirit or respect among the people they serve which challenges the caricature of faith which New Atheism promotes.

Few would dispute that secularization is happening but there are different voices arguing as to what the ways forward might be. The loss of privileged position can be seen as an opportunity for the

---

[16] Dawkins, R. (2006) *The God Delusion*. London, Toronto, Sydney, Auckland, Johannesburg: Bantam Press.

[17] Beattie, Tina (2007) *The New Atheists*. London: Darton, Longman and Todd, pp. 2–4.

Church to divest itself of ambiguities which have hampered its truly missionary and evangelical work in the past, leaving it freer to be itself rather than an uncritical supporter of the state and the status quo. The need for an effective apologetic and for leadership at all levels which can help adult Christians to be educated in their faith may prove to be an urgent need for the Church of today. Faith and reason need to be seen as natural allies rather than protagonists. On the other hand, Church leaders may have to struggle harder to make their voices heard and to have any influence on contemporary social or political policies, subject as religion is to an often hostile media. Church leaders have to earn respect and the right to be heard, not simply inherit it by virtue of their position. This requires different skills and qualities in leaders than in the past.

THE CHALLENGE TO THE CONTEMPORARY CHURCH

The Ecumenical Movement of the last century has been seen by some as a symptom of the decline of religion and the loss of those identities which were dearly argued for by great figures of the past and pursued with great energy by those who followed them. For others, the divisions within Christianity are a scandal. The achievements of the twentieth-century Ecumenical Movement have been very considerable but how are its benefits of tolerance, greater mutual understanding, sharing and liturgical convergence to be set over against the claims of a loss of confidence in knowing what your religious identity is or means? How is leadership to be exercised when different theologies, including ecclesiologies, have to be reconciled? What is legitimate diversity as against total loss of coherence due to irreconcilable opposites? Too often the history of the Church since the earliest times has been one of successive splits and schisms often done in the name of the recovery of true Christian identity and despair of the existing forms. If that path is to be abandoned, then what leadership skills will be required to hold together and embody forms of unity which can encompass difference?

The claim of Anglicanism to be able to do this has been severely tested in recent years by issues that clearly divide the Church and that some would argue have a secular agenda as their origin. Others equally maintained that issues of the position of women in the Church and of attitudes to homosexual relationships were theological problems and issues of justice that were long overdue for resolution even if this put unity under strain. The Roman Catholic Church has not been immune to internal tension either with a struggle between traditionalists and liberals over attitudes to the Second Vatican Council as well as issues arising from the handling of sexual abuse which clearly demonstrated leadership failure, especially in Ireland. History, however, may judge that all the churches were so occupied with internal issues and divisions during the last part of the twentieth century and the beginnings of the twenty-first that they were uncertain players on the world stage thus undermining the credibility of the Gospel.

A house divided against itself cannot stand but that does not necessarily argue for an intolerance of legitimate difference. Where the line is to be drawn between what can be tolerated and, indeed, even encouraged, and what clearly undermines the basic *raison d'être* of an organization is a matter of considerable debate and ecclesiological difference of view. Is the Church a collection of people who have some kind of vague loyalty to its cultural forms or is it something more than that? This is a question which again determines what kind of leadership may be needed. A key skill in leadership of the Church thus has to be the ability to forge and maintain a basic unity of thought and purpose.

Secular organizations that get this wrong go out of business, but they seem to succeed when five variables come together in the right way, i.e. good leadership, clarity of purpose, products that meet needs or desires, accessibility, and good communication to the public that the business and its products exist. How can that insight be translated into an ecclesiological form?

The dilemma has been well illustrated by Paul Avis in his book *Authority, Leadership and Conflict in the Church*[18] in which he suggests that if the Anglican Church today can be accused of a vacuum of authority, the Roman Catholic Church may be suffering from an excess of authority which actually inhibits true development in a number of key areas. He remarks sagely: 'Autocracy is not the same as leadership. Compliance is not the authentic response that we offer to true leaders,'[19] There is at least as much danger in being overconfident about answers as there is in a lack of confidence and an inability to say anything. Avis offers a threefold challenge to Anglicanism: to know itself for what it is, to know what its ministry is and to know what its Gospel is. It is a challenge to all the Christian

[18] Avis, Paul (1992) *Authority, Leadership and Conflict in the Church*. London: Mowbray.
[19] Ibid. p. 5.

churches but it must be balanced by a willingness to listen, to engage in dialogue and to adopt forms of authority that liberate creativity and active participation.

While it may be a mistake simply to speak of the Church and its leadership in these market terms, since it is open to the objection that the fact that its *product* may not be very popular, does not mean that it should cease offering it and go for another as a secular business would be tempted to do, whose prime concern is to make money for shareholders. Whether there is sufficient in the analogy for it to be worth pursuing will be explored in succeeding chapters.

The fact that we live in what is called a postmodern society under-lines that thinking in these terms may be helpful. Symbolized by the supermarket trolley, picking what one wants to believe or value at whim or by the computer screen on which a virtual reality world can be created or accessed without moving from your chair, suggests that this seems to be the world of ultimate freedom of choice. It is no coincidence that at a time of declining church affiliation, this is the age in which membership of trade unions, political parties or other movements is at an all-time low. However, it is also a time when fundamentalist groups seem able, on the other hand, to attract membership which is some cases is allied to or even involved with various forms of intolerance.

SPOILT FOR CHOICE?

For the majority of churchgoers in affluent Britain, which place of worship you go to is a choice available to most people by car and affili-ation can last simply as long as the services accord with your tastes. Except in very rural areas, allegiance to the local parish church or nearest chapel is virtually a thing of the past. If the more traditional church denominations don't suit, then there are always the house churches and other alternatives as a walk down Glastonbury High Street would quickly demonstrate. This further emphasizes that church affiliation cannot be coerced, or assumed but only freely chosen, which must mean the abandonment of leadership styles which reflect authoritarian stances of the past. Leadership has to be relational not positional.

Changes of work patterns also make traditional church attendance much more difficult. The twelve-hour shift, Sunday trading, all-night shopping, all challenge traditional rhythms which make patterns of life of even a few years ago almost impossible to sustain. Whether these changes will prove to be progress or not remains to be seen but they are certainly sea changes with which the Church is faced. Is leadership of the Church then as much about marketing as anything else?

The fall in church attendance both in the UK and in Europe has been well documented by such bodies as the Christian Research Association. Although this became very noticeable in the 1960s, it is in fact a process that was beginning to be serious in the nineteenth century also. With the exception of Pentecostalism and house church movements, most of the traditional denominations are facing serious decline. There has also been a similar decline in those who feel called to the ordained ministry, although the admission of women to it in the Protestant Churches has made an important difference to this and may also lead to creative thinking, too, about the nature of leadership. Do women bring special gifts to this? However, the numerical decline of churchgoers continues. The problem of the shortage of clergy was addressed in the Roman Catholic Church by such books as *Europe Without Priests?*[20] This was an important socio-logical, historical and theological analysis arguing for changes in practice and the adoption of different scenarios for the future, based on New Testament exegesis as well as the theology of the Second Vatican Council.

ROLE CONFUSION?

Important though this contribution was, and it was paralleled by other studies within the Catholic Church as well as by other churches,[21] it has yet to bear significant fruit. The situation that the churches are now facing stimulated contributions on the nature of ministry both within the Church of England and Methodism, for example, although latterly much of these have been as a consequence of economic considerations and concentrated on how training for the ordained ministry might be delivered rather than adopting a clear idea of what ordained and lay ministries are.[22] This lack of clarity is

[20] Kerkhofs, Jan (1995) (ed.) *Europe Without Priests?* London: SCM.

[21] In many ways Roman Catholicism was rather late on the scene in this discussion despite the relevance of important documents in Vatican II such as *Lumen Gentium* and John Paul II's Encyclical *Christifideles Laici*. See bibliography for these and other important contributions.

[22] Archbishop's Council (2003) *Formation for Ministry Within a Learning Church.* London: Church House Publishing.

by no means confined to those churches, for in 1995 Cardinal Basil Hume was to write:

> The Second Vatican Council's teaching on the priesthood began by reminding all Christians of their shared priesthood: but the essential difference in the priesthood that the Council also declared to be conferred upon bishops, presbyters and deacons by the sacrament of Holy Orders was not then made plain and has been the subject of considerable controversy and research ever since.[23]

Hume goes on to claim that this confusion over role not only led to the resignation of large numbers of ordained ministers after the Second Vatican Council but to hesitation about joining the ordained ministry at all.[24] In other words, he acknowledged that the significance of role confusion was part of the problem. The more the emphasis is on the priesthood of all, the less does the Church seem able to articulate what the ordained role is for or what kind of leadership it needs to model. Just as important is it to delineate what the priesthood of all Christians might be and what kind of leadership is appropriate for them within the Church.

This problem is well illustrated by the increasing emphasis being placed by most churches in a democratic society, on collaborative styles of leadership, which appears to echo Hutton's call for consensus and collaboration in business. Few ordained leaders in the past received any training or preparation for this and it is still mostly a low priority within ministerial training, acknowledged rather than implemented. Our context however places increasing emphasis on consultation and people having a greater say in what influences their lives. However, organizations built round consultation and collaboration require a very different style of leadership than in the past. Canon Warren writes in *A Time for Sharing*:

> Leadership for collaboration in mission will involve identifying the gifts of those within the church, and seeking to harmonize their individual (and sometimes idiosyncratic) contributions ... I believe leadership will need to avoid the disempowering style of provider/client relationship ... Collaborative ministry in mission involves going beyond allowing the laity to do what the priest has traditionally done. It is about allowing the laity to shape and be the initiators, of both their ministry and that of the clergy.[25]

[23] Foreword to Richards, Michael (1995) *A People of Priests*. London: DLT. Richards himself argued that addressing this lacuna was now urgent.

[24] Ibid.

[25] London Church House (1995) *A Time for Sharing – Collaborative Ministry in Mission*, Board of Mission Occasional Paper No. 6. London: Church House Publishing, pp. 25–26. cf also the Roman Catholic Report published in the same year, *The Sign We Give*. Bishops

Reservations about this stance came not just from clergy and laity who find such ideas threatening, but also from a theological perspective which indicates that there are differences of view, which need to be worked through, about the nature of the ordained priesthood as well as how far we can be influenced by models of working derived from other spheres of life. As one writer has put it: 'Some of us are profoundly disturbed by trends within the Church which seem to imitate questionable features of the world at large'.[26]

One response to this might be that, on the contrary, collaborative styles of working are more consonant with the New Testament and that it is the more hierarchical models that really derive from secular life, as it was understood at the time of the Emperor Constantine and which became so influential during the Middle Ages.

This underlines that there is a need to clarify the roles of clergy and laity and ground them ecclesiologically and highlights the fact that, if these new ways of working are to be implemented, they will have profound implications for how we describe and make real, ministry within and on behalf of the Church, to which we will return. The Church has to become predominantly relational and a place of mutual trust in collaborative endeavour.

However in many ways, these studies do not take sufficient account of the underlying contextual situation which seems to have caught the Church in Europe and the UK on the back foot and may contribute to this confusion and lack of clarity.

History has shown that leadership in the Church has evolved and its theology with it. Many of the reasons for this were contextual as the Church responded to or was heavily influenced by the secular circumstances of a given historical period. Some changes were pragmatic as the Church grew and became more complex and institutional, but other developments are a result of a developing ecclesiology; how the Church viewed itself in the light of the Gospel and its mission. It was often the case that these factors were so intermingled that separating them out is very difficult, complicated by the fact that in the Early Church especially, there was more variety of practice than has often been presupposed.[27]

Conference of England and Wales, London 1995, which equally emphasized this point adding this was part of the meaning of being a Church community which is a bearer of the Gospel. It is an issue of ecclesiology not just of effectiveness as judged by secular criteria.

[26] The contribution of Richard Oakley in *A Time for Sharing* (1995) p. 30.

[27] Hill, E. (1988) *Ministry and Authority in the Catholic Church.* London: Chapman. Edmund Hill summarizes the development of ministry during the first millennium, see Chapter 3, pp. 32ff.

The temptation to appeal to a universal paradigm that can be regarded as normative should, therefore, be resisted which is not to deny that there are important pointers to be found in biblical literature and in tradition.

How, then, are we to move forward? The need to be faithful to the Gospel will require here a profound insight both into the Church's roots but also an ability to discern the signs for the times and to bring these together in an appropriate way.

WELLS OF WISDOM

The Christian Church, perhaps unlike all other organizations, draws from a number of different *wells* when thinking about its life and mission or when planning change. These are:

- Revelation.
- Reason, including theological insights from the past and present.
- Experience of the contemporary church and its context.
- Secular knowledge.
- Authority.

Different traditions within the Christian Church will emphasize some more than others and may also interpret them differently, but any consideration of how leadership is to be exercised today will require thinking theologically as well as organizationally, hence all these *wells* will need to be visited, although the one marked *Revelation* will clearly be foundational. A model of how this might be done will be explored in a later chapter but any new models of leadership need to be well grounded theologically and be organizationally feasible, rather than the outcome of economics or mere expediency. In doing this, issues of the nature and role of the Church, of mission, of the meaning of ministry as well as how these *wells* of wisdom be used, need be brought coherently together. Leadership is a theological issue for the Church because it must be rooted in Christ and the Gospel and be a vehicle which expresses this. Leadership is a fundamental aspect of the Church as sign to the world.

Christianity is incarnational because it accepts that God became part of human history in Christ; to disregard the faith that comes to us from Revelation is to treat the Church as if it is a purely secular organization and to ignore the perspectives of the Kingdom and the vocation of Christians to make this real in the life of their world. However, to rely solely on the source(s) of faith is to ignore the real insights of men and women living now and the gifts that God has given all humans to search for and find truth in their lives and to reflect on that. Bringing these together frees the Church from enslavement to precedent enabling it to discover new ways of being which are faithful to Christian origins but also open to fresh expressions of the Gospel. To be a living church means not merely repeating or replicating what has been the practice in the past but innovating also. The role of authority is to be the servant of this process as well as to regulate it purposefully and authentically.

The parables of the seeds found in the Synoptic Gospels illustrate this very well. Seeds contain messages from the past, their DNA, which determine what kind of living thing they will become, but this is not mere replication. Seeds become plants and grow in response to climate, soil and nurture. They also evolve over time as successive generations respond to their environment. In this sense, perhaps, leadership can be seen as a form of imaginative cultivation, of trusteeship in covenant, with the prime purpose of enabling new growth to be vigorous and productive as well as suitable for its locale; rooted in the past, responding to the present, and open to the future. Successful leadership requires some of the skills of the discerning farmer who knows how to bring together and harness the different factors which are essential for strong plant growth.

The metaphor of seeds and sowing can be pressed further. Cultivation is only successful with the right seeds, planted at the right time, in the right way and in the right soil which has been carefully prepared. The sower needs therefore to have both knowledge and skill but, as we have seen, what knowledge and which skills is a pragmatic problem requiring discernment of the context in which the Church now finds itself. It is also an ecclesiological one as it finds new ways of fulfilling its basic and fundamentally unchanging purpose. It also has to be learnt and practised.

Thus there are two kinds of theology which can be found to be present in the contemporary Church which might be described as 'Seed Theology' and 'Script Theology'. 'Seed Theology' follows evolutionary insights and seeks under the guidance of the Spirit to be true to the narratives of the past but open to developing forms in the future that can be grown and nurtured, whereas 'Script Theology' denies this, suggesting that the only way forward is by simply replicating the past, ignoring the lessons of history as well as the present; learning the past, not learning from the past. This does not lead to growth or new life and is, in effect, the fundamentalist option.

Many people therefore would argue that, given the present position of Christianity in the northern hemisphere, we need to develop the skills and gifts of the Church community as never before and that new ways of being church must urgently be explored. Simply replicating past models is not an option but neither is abandoning our roots and the wisdom of the past. This will be explored further when considering the leadership and management of change. What is needed, however, in thinking about the future shape and configuration of the Church is profound discernment and analysis of our context and how the Gospel of Christ is to be made present within it and then to respond by developing appropriate forms of leadership that spring from a coherent 'Seed Theology' of what the Church is and what it is about. No religious body can hope to continue without such a theology that is internally consistent, credible to its members and intelligible to others. Such leadership must be faithful to what the Church is, as well as responsive to the context in which it is found. Mere replication is not an option, but neither is unreflective innovation.[28] Different kinds of leadership in the Church will be needed at varying times and places depending on circumstances, for no one size fits all, but there are also important general things that can be said about the nature of church leadership itself which the chapters that follow will explore. There has, perhaps, never been a time when the task has been more urgent.

Consensus leadership

Much of recent church history of most of the denominations has been characterized by polarizations which threaten its unity. The General Election of 2010 produced a hung Parliament and a coalition which, faced with dire economic problems, provided the opportunity for consensus politics in the national interest which set on one side narrow party interests. History will tell whether or not this will be a success but it represents a way forward from which leaders in the churches could well learn. Paul warned the Corinthian Church of the dangers of rivalry and petty loyalties (1 Cor. 3.3-16), reminding

---

[28] This raises the important question of how the Church discerns authentic development from what is spurious. J. H. Newman attempted to resolve this by his *Essay on the Development of Christian Doctrine* in which he wrote 'if Christianity be a universal religion, suited not to one locality or period, but to all times and places, it cannot but vary in its relations and dealings towards the world around it'. *An Essay on the Development of Christian Doctrine*, Longmans (standard edn), p. 58.

them that it is God's work that they should be about which is founded in Jesus Christ, as stewards entrusted with the mysteries of God (1 Cor. 4.1) and not people filled with their own self-importance. The consensus of which Paul speaks is more than just a workable compromise, important though that is, but living from and united by the Gospel which is foolishness to the world. This requires the leadership to foster unity by showing constantly what it means to be rooted in Christ and to be a pattern for that, exhibiting more than merely human principles and standards. It is in this way that leadership in the Church should be similar to the best examples of society today but also radically different.

QUESTIONS

- What do you see as the signs of the times today and how do you interpret them?
- What should be the main role of the Church in society in the twenty-first century? Are the images of *salt* and *leaven* helpful?
- What seeds of ho can you identify and how can they be grown and nurtured?
- In what ways can the laity be encouraged to shape ministry in the Church?
- Do we need more consensus leadership in today's Church? If so, how can that be achieved?

Chapter 2

ECCLESIOLOGY AND MISSION

Being a church leader in the modern world is not easy, and this may account to some extent for a lack of vocations to ordained leadership in recent times. The Church has some major internal challenges that need to be resolved if church leaders are to be effective and achieve their aims. One of them, although not obvious but perhaps the greatest, is the lack of consistent ecclesiology. British Methodism is in some turmoil over this as it struggles to find its vocation for the twenty-first century. Although Catholicism was energized by Vatican II, there is still debate, revisionism and inner struggle for a way forward, and the Anglican Church openly admits to having those within it who see a distinctive Anglican ecclesiology as possible and those who don't. Perhaps the Anglican *fudge* is best seen in its mission. Its mission initiative, fresh expressions, has raised a debate as to how to live with the status quo model of a pastoral ministry that Anglicanism has enjoyed since the Reformation, and a missionary model. It has been expressed as the difference between a theology which sees the God of mission forming a church, and the Church of God engaged in a mission. In the first, mission dictates the shape of church, as in the content of the Anglican report *Mission Shaped Church*. In the second, the Church is tasked with mission.

The church leader is, of course, caught up in all this, and the confusion can be a cause of powerful influence, if not stress. What is needed is a clearer view of the shape of the Church based on some parameters of classical ecclesiology and a way forward for mission ambitions to be realized more fully.

ECCLESIOLOGY AND VOCATION

The word *ecclesiology* has its root in the notion of vocation. An *ecclesia*, in a broad sense, is an assembly that is called to be and become something. To discover the nature of ecclesiology is to discover in what ways a group of people are called, and what ontology and purposes they are called to fulfil. All ecclesiologies will grapple with these questions and answers might be found in common and unique ways. The utilization of a secular concept (*ekklesia*) to form the basis of a religious construct epitomizes the challenge involved in describing categories for ecclesiology.[1] Moltmann makes this clear when he speaks of the Church's responsibilities:

> The Church will always have to present itself both in the forum of God and in the forum of the world. For it stands for God to the world, and it stands for the world before God. It confronts the world in critical liberty and is bound to give it the authentic revelation of the new life.[2]

The Church is obligated to inhabit the world of the everyday. It is visible, rooted and to some extent seemingly unconcerned about borrowing secular language and concepts. And yet it also claims to be transcendent, invisible and given life from above. The dynamic forces of ecclesiology are found in a dichotomy. The Church claims to be both a visible entity and an invisible eschatological reality. This may at first suggest a rich variety of form, which indeed it offers, but it also highlights the epistemological challenge when considering a particular ecclesiology.

WHAT ARE THE COMPONENTS OF ECCLESIOLOGY?

Like any discipline, some fundamental questions can be asked of ecclesiology. What is its essential nature and what constitutes it? What is its purpose and what is it designed to do? What does it have and use to fulfil its purpose and how is it organized? This tripod of questions will define, give direction and reveal the resources ecclesiology relies on, for, like many disciplines, ecclesiology is composite. The nature of its practice is dependent on the constellation of the components within its remit. To investigate the nature of ecclesiology is to discover

---

[1] Schillebeeckx outlines how *ekklesia* was a gathering of Roman citizens. Schillebeeckx, E. (1996), *Church: The Human Story of God*, trans. by John Bowden. New York: Crossroad Publishing, p. 146.

[2] Moltmann, J. (1977) *The Church in the Power of the Spirit*, trans. by Margaret Kohl. London: SCM Press, p. 1.

the field or scope of its enquiry by means of understanding a range of components. The components can suggest varying starting points. Ecclesiology therefore, can be approached from different viewpoints and disciplines. The context of such perspectives will likely include notions of theologies of ministry, ordination, laity, ecumenism and mission. The issues raised may also enquire into models of authority, sources of truth and how the processes of revelation find coherence. Underlying this, a local church will likely exhibit some visible hallmarks and hold some tenets which define its nature and purpose. These are some of the elements of what is normally known as an ecclesiology or doctrine of the Church and are worth further examination when considering an evaluation of any given ecclesiology.

Paul Avis offers the clearest definition of the components of ecclesiology in his editorial Foreword to *The Christian Church*.[3] He suggests that the contributors to the edition deal with questions to do with theological claims and authoritative sources such as Scripture, tradition and reason. They outline councils, historic formularies, the nature of the Church and its mission. Structures of ministry and leadership, communion and fellowship, and the ecumenical future of the unity of all churches are also described. In a sense he is delimiting ecclesiology as a discipline. Other ecclesiologists focus their views on the particular. For instance, David Edwards, in *What is Catholicism?* makes a critique of the Church on the historic ordering of ordained leaders, governance through a primate and councils, and sources of truth.[4] Robin Greenwood enlists Boff, Gunton, Moltman and Zizioulas to form an appeal for an Anglican ecclesiology predicated on relational theology.[5] Zizioulas also envisages the Eucharistic community as the prime context of the Church.[6] Avery Dulles employs a metaphorical approach when he orders ecclesiology by use of models such as sacrament, mystical communion, herald, institution and servant.[7] Hans Küng roots his ecclesiological work in biblical studies, especially in the New Testament, before offering insights from the *notae ecclesiae* of the Church.[8] Miroslav Volf, contrasts the

[3] Avis, P. (ed.) (2002), *The Christian Church: An Introduction to the Major Traditions*. London: SPCK, pp. ix–xiii.

[4] Edwards, D. L. (1994) *What is Catholicism?* London: Mowbray, pp. 39–86.

[5] Greenwood, R. (1994) *Transforming Priesthood*. London: SPCK, p. 82.

[6] Zizioulas, J. D. (1985) *Being As Communion*. London: Darton, Longman & Todd, pp. 143–169.

[7] Dulles, A. (2002) *Models of the Church* (ext. edn). New York: Doubleday, pp. 26–94.

[8] Küng, H. (1968) *The Church*. London: Search Press, pp. 43–104, 263–359.

work of Ratzinger and Zizioulas and discusses Catholic and Orthodox views concerning hierarchical structures.[9] From this he advocates a model for the local church as an assembly.

Therefore, ecclesiology utilizes a series of component and formularies that describe its nature, hopes, aspirations, purpose and organization. All these will employ a variety of theological disciplines: historical theology, biblical studies, authority and leadership, metaphorical theology, missiology and relational theology. These form the essential components of any given ecclesiology and can generally be described as either Faith or Order elements. Faith elements derive from faith statements, being the formulation of that which is experienced by the followers of Christianity. Order elements derive from applied theologies, organizational influences, historical contingency and metaphorical models.

ECCLESIOLOGY AS DEFINED BY FAITH STATEMENTS

The Church cannot simply be described in organizational terms. The faith of leaders and members has shaped it through its life and this shaping process has sometimes been written and captured in texts. Under the heading *Faith Statement*, a suggested text begins to present itself. The *notes* (sometimes called *marks*) of the Church found in the Nicene Creed, revealing something of the Church's nature can be used to examine the ontology of the Church. Oneness, holiness, catholicity and apostolicity have historically described the nature of church. In its visible and earthly form, the degree to which particular notes predominate configures the distinctiveness of one expression of church from another, yet they also have the potential to express a common eschatological reality. In terms of their overall influence, Robin Greenwood writes in *Transforming Priesthood* that the *notes* of the Church have been monopolized by Catholics and given low profile by Protestants. Even if Greenwood is right, perhaps in the ecumenical and eclectic contemporary scene there is still value in comparing any given ecclesiology, which sees itself as both reformed and Catholic, with the *notes*.

For this, the ecclesiologist Hans Küng, whom Adrian Hastings recognizes as having played a significant part in the formation of

[9] Volf, M. (1998) *After Our Likeness.* Cambridge: William B. Eerdmanns Publishing Company, p. 123.

English Christian theology,[10] (although it has to be said a sporadic role in Roman Catholic ecclesiology) is a prominent source. Küng is clear and succinct in his definitions. As a teacher and writer he has proven experience as an academic. He is also an ecumenist. This is important as Greenwood outlines:

> To belong to a particular church today is not a matter of defending a single ecclesiology and doctrine of ministry in a polemical engagement with others. Rather it is to recognize that the particular self-definition of one church occurs partly and simultaneously though an open and continuing process of learning from others.[11]

THE NOTES OF THE CHURCH ACCORDING TO KÜNG

This seminal concept of *One, Holy, Catholic and Apostolic Church* was etched out of the groundwork of the first four centuries of Christian life and debate. It was known in the Church since its birth, but was formularized, reaffirmed and improved in the four great Councils of Nicea, Constantinople, Ephesus and Chalcedon. Küng describes their historic evolution as originating and developing from polemical defences of the faith in Ignatius, Irenaeus, Clement, Tertullian, Cyprian and Augustine.[12] In order to understand them better, his analysis of the individual parts is as follows.

One

Küng defines oneness ontologically as unity in diversity, and pragmatically as involving the reunion of the churches by necessity. In terms of unity in diversity, he claims that the New Testament is clear that unity does not mean uniformity. The point he makes is that unity is derived from above. It is a spiritual entity, not management of individuals or groups in order to create a whole. In terms of the reunion of the churches he notes how this is prone to various evasions; division simply regarded as a norm or a retreat from any visible disunity. However, he suggests ways in which unity can be rediscovered, suggesting that:

- The existing common ecclesial reality must be recognized.
- The desired common ecclesial reality must be found.

---

[10] Hastings, A. (1986) *A History of English Christianity 1920–2000*, (4th edn) London: SCM Press, p. 663.

[11] Greenwood, R. *Transforming Priesthood.* p. 111.

[12] Küng, H. *The Church*, p. 266.

- Work for unity must start in one's own church, but with the other churches in mind.
- Truth must not be sacrificed, but rediscovered.
- The Gospel of Jesus Christ is taken as the standard for unity as a whole.

Holy

He goes to some length to make it clear that he is writing of a real church not an idealized version of an ecclesiology. While the Church's holiness is in being set apart by God, yet in reality it is still sinful in many respects. Because of this it is in need of reconciliation. These two facts cannot be separated, just like an individual may recognize two sides of their being, one sinful and the other good. It is not possible to cut one off. He contrasts the view of the Church from above, embraced by the holiness of God, and from below, caught in the sinfulness of the world. The Church must not deny either its eschatological privilege or its place in the world. Any retreat towards the invisibility of the Church fails to take its purpose seriously.

Catholic

Catholicity is limited because he says the New Testament does not refer directly to the Church as catholic. Clearly in his view, catholicity was damaged by the Reformation in a similar way as was unity, and he recognizes the same responses to recover it. The first is to resort to the notion of the invisible church, where catholicity is perfected. His point is that speculation about true catholicity becomes possible at the *parousia*. This eschatological treatment is then characteristically balanced by an explanation of how it relates to incarnational theology. Nothing of spatial extensity, numerical quantity, cultural variety or temporal continuity can make the church catholic. Catholicity is not a geographical, statistical, sociological or historical construct. None of these things are excluded from it but they do not constitute it. They are transcended by catholicity. It is an all-embracing ecumenical identity which makes the church catholic. In essence it does not bow to the pressures of the world, nor veer from its given course. It remains true to orthodoxy, interpreting it for each generation.

Apostolic

In his exploration of apostolicity he asserts that it is within the apostles' witness and mission that the Church finds its purpose. What the apostles regarded as the task and commission given them by

Christ has become the task of the Church. For the Church, apostolic obedience is to follow the apostles:

> Apostolic succession is therefore a question of a continual and living confrontation of the Church and all its members with this apostolic witness; apostolic succession is fulfilled when this witness is heard, respected, believed, confessed and followed.[13]

He identifies that to do this the Church needs two things: to remain open to the Spirit, and to discern the apostolic witness through the writings of the New Testament and the Hebrew scriptures, for only then will it find obedience. What makes Küng's description focused is that he combines the need to be both theologically aware of the apostolic tradition as well as engaged in a contemporary living witness. This is useful to any evaluation of educational and missionary proposals, in that an analysis will look for their theological derivation, ambition and integrity, as well as consonance with a living witness in their contemporary contexts.

ECCLESIOLOGY AS DEFINED BY ORDER

Order, as suggested above, is the way a church expresses its vocation through applied theologies, organization, history and modelling.

Applied theologies

Because ecclesiology is concerned with the people who constitute the Church, it will naturally be concerned with both members and leaders. This means that theologies of ordination and laity will be important. A theology of ordination will describe the vocation, equipping, responsibility and authority of a leader. For example, the inclusion of an episcopal role in the Church, noted in Volf's contention above, argues for an ecclesiology governed by an assembly rather than a bishop. Some Churches ordain and preserve a permanent diaconate and in others the diaconate is a transitional period. A theology of ordination will seek to expose the reasons, biblical and theological, behind its practices.

A theology of laity will clearly make certain demands on the laity but, as Yves Congar was aware,[14] it will also define priesthood. The relationship between clergy and laity will need careful definition.

---

[13] Küng, H. *The Church*, p. 356.

[14] Congar, Y. (1957) *Lay People in the Church*, trans. Donald Attwater. London: Bloomsbury Publishing, p. xxxi.

Laos is a term which embraces the whole of the people of God and consequently an interesting paradox appears. As leaders are part of the membership, it is also true therefore, that ordained people are part of the laity. This means that a theology of laity will need to address how leaders relate to the whole people of God. Conversely, laity is defined in the New Testament as a priesthood,[15] which raises the question of how this priesthood is to be exercised in relation to the ordained. It is interesting to note that in the Roman Catholic Church a man is 'ordained to priesthood in the presbyteral order' whereas in the Anglican ordinal the terms 'priest' and 'presbyter' are interchangeable, and there is no reference in the title to an order.

Considering the more familiar definition of laity, those who are not ordained, which is the generally accepted sense of the term, a theology of laity will also need to address how lay people find and exercise their vocation in the Church and world, how they may contribute to the overall governance of the Church, and how they are encouraged to contribute to the theology of the Church. For example, John MacQuarrie, in *The Faith of the People of God*, proposes a lay theology of, by and for the people of God. His thesis is that this 'will lean toward the apologetic type'.[16] Jeff Astley advocates research into lay theology which he entitles *Ordinary Theology*,[17] meaning the theology that lay people understand and receive, rather than that which leaders teach. Each is an example of a construct of a theology of laity derived from, or leading to a specific ecclesiology.

Beyond theologies of ordination and laity, a satisfactory ecclesiology will also embrace theologies of ministry and mission. Avis explores the pivotal connection between them and suggests that to distinguish them too much may, in fact be unhelpful. [18] He suggests that it might be better to affirm them as ministry in mission, emphasizing the pastoral heart of outreach.[19] However, caution needs to be exercised, as to blur the distinction too much can leave both mission and ministry devoid of meaning.

A theology of ministry must investigate how the ordained and non-ordained members of the Church fulfil their vocation. If, as Avis suggests, ordained leaders are the enablers and supporters of the

[15] I Peter 2. 5.

[16] Macquarrie, J. (1972) *The Faith of the People of God: A Lay Theology*. London: SCM Press, pp. 1–8.

[17] Astley, J. (2002) *Ordinary Theology*. Aldershot: Ashgate Publishing, pp. 97–122.

[18] Avis, P. (2005) *A Ministry Shaped by Mission*. London: T&T Clark, pp. 1–87.

[19] Avis, P. (2003) *A Church Drawing Near*. London: T&T Clark, pp. 180–200.

ministry of the Church, then it will seek to offer offices which will express the faith of the Church as a totality. A theology of ministry will also clarify the status of charisms and define how pneumatology contributes to the overall theology of gifts. For example Congar's pneumatological Christology demonstrates how charisms are based on the double constitution of Christ as *Servant-Messiah* (shown in his baptism), and *Lord* (shown at his resurrection and exaltation).[20] A satisfactory ecclesiology will attempt to hold together, allow dialogue and find interpretation within these theologies.

In this dialectical sense of ecclesiology, various insights enrich the Church and lead towards a theology of the sources of truth and authority that are necessary components of coherence. Sources of truth will seek to answer the epistemological questions of constituting the Church in terms of hermeneutical process. Authority will attempt to determine how issues of governance and discipline are enacted. Theologies in these areas will consider the issues of power, responsibility and accountability. Avis offers some explanation of the differences between various forms of power and suggests that sources of truth and authority often form processes by which the organization of the Church and much of its activities rest.[21] Stephen Sykes warns that issues such as these need careful examination for the abuse of power and authority is a major factor in the practice of the Church today. He advocates examining Gregory's Pastoral Care as 'exceptionally instructive'.[22] From this it is clear that various applied theologies lie beneath the visible form of the Church supporting, or perhaps challenging, the practical life of it. Another factor that can add or reduce the success of the Church is the complex structure of its organization.

Organizational structure

The Church is, in part, a group of people who regularly gather for activities such as worship, learning, engaging with issues of community, mutual nurture, planning, managing and decision making. Because of this, it is a social entity that can, like any other group, be subject to various forms of sociology and social engineering.

---

[20] Congar, Y. (1999) *I Believe in the Holy Spirit*, trans. by David Smith (3 volumes, Vol. 3). New York: The Crossroad Publishing Company, pp. 165–173.

[21] Avis, P. (1992) *Authority, Leadership and Conflict in the Church*. London: Mowbray, pp. 7–15 and 19–25.

[22] Sykes, S. (2006) *Power and Christian Theology*. London: Continuum International Publishing, pp. 135–152 (142).

An early (1927) sociological exploration into the relationship of society and religion can be found in Bonhoeffer's doctoral dissertation, *Sanctorum Communio*, co-titled *A Dogmatic Inquiry into the Sociology of the Church.* Here he contrasts religious community with the concept of the Kingdom of God, arguing that they can easily be confused, leading to a misunderstanding of what the Church really is. He defines it thus: 'It is in the necessary bond between the basic relationships and the empirical form of community as a special form that the nature of the Church, formally speaking, resides'.[23] Using Max Scheler, he denotes four forms of expression of community and basic relationships; mystic, associational, collectivist, and communal.[24] Essentially he defined sociological categories of how a group relates to the internal and external agendas in its context, and what stimuli shape its community.

This insight, possibly quite acceptable today to contemporary leaders of the Church in terms of its categories, might not have been accepted just a few years ago. Indeed, Joseph McCann, in *Church and Organisation*,[25] comments that seeking to relate religion, sociology and the Church led to controversy in the last decades of the twentieth century. Sociologists who sought to analyze the Church from the point of view of a social structure were accused of sociological reductionism. However, as Robin Gill states in the introduction to *Theology and Sociology:*

> The first edition of this book tried to reflect a remarkable change that took place within academic theology in the 1970s and early 1980s. After years of neglect, theologians and biblical scholars started to take sociology seriously, to read the classical studies of Weber, Durkheim and Troeltsch, and to lose some of their old fears.[26]

However, Milbank calls the sociological project into question and provides a critique of the theological and anti-theological scientific enterprise of sociology. In the final chapter of *Theology & Social Theory*, he proposes that in fact theology itself can provide what is required and be thought of as social science:

> There can only be a distinguishable Christian social theory because there is also a distinguishable Christian mode of action, a definite practice. The theory (the assertion that theology is itself a social science) explicates this practice,

[23] Bonhoeffer, D. (1963) [1930] *Sanctorum Communio: A Dogmatic Enquiry into the Sociology of the Church*, trans. by R. Gregor Smith. London: Collins, p. 87.

[24] Bonhoeffer, D. *Sanctorum Communio*, pp. 86–97.

[25] McCann, J. F. (1993) *Church and Organisation: A Sociological and Theological Enquiry.* London: Associated University Press, pp. 20–33.

[26] Gill, R. (ed.) (1996) *Theology and Sociology: A Reader.* London: Cassell, p. 2.

which arose in certain precise historical circumstances, and exists only as a particular historical development. The theory therefore, is first and foremost an ecclesiology, and only an account of other human societies to the extent that the Church defines itself, in its practice, as in continuity and discontinuity with these societies.[27]

Gill's hypothesis is interesting when he describes some approaches to a sociological interpretation of church under the headings of interactionist, functionalist and relationalist theory. Each has its own interpretative method and is distinguished from the others. Although it is not possible to explicate a full description of purpose and methodology here, in brief, the interactionist approach employs a survey of how the Church influences and is influenced by society. Functionalists interpret the Church from origins stemming from characteristic behaviours, and relationalists, such as Troeltsch and H. Richard Niebuhr examine the relationship between the Church and society. This third methodology will feature later in a consideration of the Church and culture.

Recent theological training has begun to use managerial concepts, group dynamics, leadership practice, social theory, and other disciplines to aid the organizational structure of the Church. This has been taken much more seriously over recent years. It is not uncommon in theological colleges for potential leaders to read the work of a host of authors including Meredith Belbin, Stephen Pattison, Charles Handy, Donald Schön, John Adair and Eric Berne. Not all of these, of course, are outright advocates of managerial practices.[28]

Although organizational structure is heavily dependent on the insights of sociological constructs and this is not to do solely with authority and leadership, it is clear that authority structures and regimes, and the powers exerted by leadership are paramount to the shaping of any organization or ecclesiology. This is very much the case in terms of hegemony. Charles Handy, in *Gods of Management*, although not written overtly for church leaders, offers some innovative thinking formed from his observations of Greek god types. In his earlier work *Understanding Organisations*, he also provides helpful insights about how leaders and managers can understand and contribute to change in organizations. The point is that these

---

[27] Milbank, J. (1990) *Theology & Social Theory*. Oxford: Blackwell, p. 380, (my brackets, emphasis in original).

[28] For example see Pattison, S. (1997) *The Faith of the Managers: When Management Becomes Religion*. London: Cassell, pp. 140–144. In particular, he offers a fair assessment of Charles Handy.

are insights borrowed from the secular world which might be used in church growth and the reshaping of the Church, highlighting the dichotomy the Church faces in being in the world but not of it.

Historical contingency

Some ecclesiologists begin their explorations from an historical perspective, which inevitably means an emphasis on its visibility. Melinsky, for example, traces the early origins of the Church in England through the first centuries in *formational* terms leading to *deformation* at the end of the fourth century and *reformation* at the beginning of the sixteenth.[29] Other authors offer a similar approach. Williams' locates major figures of the Church of England in an historical treatment. He selects Tyndale, Hooker, Herbert, Westcott, Michael Ramsey and Robinson. Each is described to provide an understanding of their contribution to the identity of the Anglican Church.[30] Kerr provides a similar approach for the Roman Catholic Church over the period of the twentieth century.[31] His project is to map the progress of Neo-scholasticism during the period, and he portrays the biography and contribution of great Roman Catholic theologians such as Congar, Schillebeeckx, Rahner and von Balthasar. Avis' major volume *Anglicanism and the Christian Church* outlines the contributions of Anglican exponents in detail from the Reformation to the present day. His historical modelling enables him to hypothesize that Anglicanism has passed through two significant periods in terms of its governance, Erastian and apostolic, which has influenced its direction and progress.[32] It now inhabits a third, that of communion-through-baptism which draws it towards a greater ecumenism. Ecclesiology takes note of the historical paradigm in which it exists and the evolution which has enabled it to achieve its contemporary location.

Hanson and Hanson explore biblical history using Barth, and state that although 'there is not in the New Testament any formal institution

---

[29] Melinsky, M. A. H. (1992) *The Shape of the Ministry.* Norwich: The Canterbury Press, pp. 3–123.

[30] Williams, R. (2004) *Anglican Identities.* London: Darton, Longman & Todd, pp. 9–120.

[31] Kerr, F. (2007) *Twentieth Century Catholic Theologians.* Oxford: Blackwell, pp. 17–202.

[32] Avis, P. (2002) *Anglicanism and the Christian Church,* (revised and expanded edn.). Edinburgh: T & T Clark, pp. 335–354.

or founding of the Church',[33] the predominant understanding is that Christ inaugurated the renewed people of God. They acknowledge that this is refuted by Catholic theologians and quote Mersch and *Lumen Gentium* which see the Church established by Christ sending his apostles and appointing Peter over them. Edwards debates this interpretation,[34] arguing that the misuse of the word *apostolos* as a *college* which, under Peter, is organized as an entity, confuses ecclesiology. The visibility of the Church is discussed in depth by Butler who advocates with Luther, that the 'Church, thought primarily and even essentially invisible is nevertheless involved in history and thus acquires a contingent and variable visibility'.[35]

The point about historical ecclesiology is that within it lies philosophical categories, such as those in Kerr, paradigmatic categories as in Avis and Melinsky, biographical categories as in Williams, hegemonic categories as in Edwards and biblical categories as in Hanson and Hanson and these listed here are not exhaustive. This gives rise to widely differing emphasizes across denominations and expressions. Each denomination must live with its historical contingency and decide how to employ it. As Greenwood argues, churches in late modernity must not only learn from other churches, but also 'relate to each other's different eras of time'.[36]

Models of church

A highly influential work in the West in recent times is Avery Dulles' *Models of Church*. Dulles orders his ecclesiology by use of metaphorical models: sacrament, mystical communion, herald, institution, servant. He argues:

> I wish to indicate my conviction that the Church, like other theological realities, is a mystery. Mysteries are realities of which we cannot speak directly. If we wish to talk about them at all we must draw on analogies afforded by our experience of the world. These analogies provide models. By attending to the analogies and utilizing them as models, we can grow in our understanding of the Church.[37]

---

[33] Hanson, A. T. & Hanson, R. P. C, (1987) *The Identity of the Church*. London: SCM Press, pp. 1–22.

[34] Edwards, D. L. *What is Catholicism?*, p. 54.

[35] Butler, B. C. (1962) *The Idea of the Church*. London: Darton, Longman & Todd, pp. 13–15.

[36] Greenwood, R. *Transforming Priesthood*, p. 110.

[37] Dulles, A. *Models of Church*, p. 2.

The use of metaphors and models is well known in theology. In Sallie McFague's *Metaphorical Theology* she states:

> In the continuum of religious language from primary, imagistic to secondary, conceptual, a form emerges which is a mixed type: *the model.* The simplest way to define a model is as a dominant metaphor, a metaphor with staying power. Metaphors are usually the work of an individual, a flash of insight which is often passing. But some metaphors gain wide appeal and become major ways of structuring and ordering experience.[38]

Models have gained wide appeal in the Church. Yvonne Craig describes the Church of England by use of three financial metaphors.[39] An Anglican version of *Models of Church* (following Dulles?), was explored by Michael Nazir-Ali, an Anglican bishop, in his attempt to formulate an ecclesiology for the new millennium.[40] Other contributors to metaphorical models of church include Paul Minear[41] and Geoffrey Preston.[42] Models and metaphors are clearly important to ecclesiology. However, Dulles cautions that models employed uncritically make the Church what they decided it was in the first place. Nevertheless, McFague's remarks suggest a positive use for them if they enable invisible constructs to be represented. This in turn can lead to the facilitation of church growth and development.

Four dimensions – applied theologies, organizational structures, historical contingencies and metaphorical models – are composite forms for ecclesiology. Applied theologies of church are crucial in determining the operation of ecclesiology. A lack of clarity or coherence will likely impair the functionality of the Church. Sociological insight can be helpful in the construction of the organizational aspects of church. It can sometimes also offer a diagnosis of problems. Historical contingencies can determine future courses of action which therefore need conscious efforts of reflection to enable good uses of past actions. Models of church also need to be handled reflectively and critically in order to bring structure as well

---

[38] McFague, S. (1983) *Metaphorical Theology.* London: SCM Press, p. 23, (emphasis in original).

[39] Craig, Y. (1996) *Tomorrow is Another Country*, GS misc. 467. London: Church House Publishing, pp. 52–57.

[40] The images of 'body', 'communion', 'pilgrim' and 'learning community' are particularly explored in Nazir-Ali, M. (2001) *Shapes of the Church to Come.* Eastbourne: Kingsway Publications, pp. 84–102.

[41] See Minear, P. S. (1961) *Images of the Church in the New Testament.* London: Lutterworth Press, pp. 28–220.

[42] See Preston, G. OP, (1997) *Faces of the Church.* Edinburgh: T&T Clark.

as development. An overall ecclesiology will need to define how these components cohere and relate. Only then will a sufficient description of ecclesiology have become possible in order to know what models of mission are available. The theology of mission or missiology will differ depending on the cultural influences of the Church, on the resources available, and also on the shape of church. Christ called his disciples into a community, an act of mission which would then continue his mission. God's church was born out of the missionary call of Christ – note that ecclesia means called out. It was called to be something, and the something is the Church, which in turn needs to become the missionary conduit of calling to others.

MISSION

One of the foremost recent missiologists, David Bosch provides an analysis of a biblical foundation for mission in his book *Transforming Mission*.[43] He outlines three paradigms – Matthean, Lukan and Pauline. This highlights three main missionary statements of the New Testament, namely the Great Commission in Matthew 28.16-20 which is centred on proclamation, the Lukan manifesto in Luke 4.16-21 which portrays the need for forgiveness, and solidarity with the poor, and the Pauline imperative to the ministry of reconciliation seen in various parts of Paul, but perhaps summarized in 2 Corinthians 5 and 6. It also explicates the diverse and complex methodology and theology of mission found in Paul's writing. What is gained by Bosch's paradigms? At a foundational level he reveals a set of biblical components that define mission, including the work of the Spirit initiating and guiding, encountering and living the resurrection and building resurrection communities. These pneumatological issues are vital to consider. The lack of them forms significant damage to a subsequent ecclesiology. What is also gained by Bosch's analysis is the basis for a definition of mission consisting of four main components. Mission is a fusion of God's action (missio dei), the fostering of individual human qualities (Christian anthropology), the life and fellowship of believers (Eucharistic community), and the deliberate actions of the community (ethical mores).[44]

At one level, defining mission is fairly straightforward. It means *being sent*, from its Latin origin, however, who is sent, how they go,

[43] Bosch, D. J. (1991) *Transforming Mission: Paradigm Shifts in Theology of Mission.* New York: Orbis, pp. 15–178.

[44] Bosch, D. J. (1991) *Transforming Mission,* pp. 368–507.

what they might do and what the result of the enterprise might be is more complex. A definition can be approached from a number of perspectives. Hoekendijk, a European missiologist, expresses mission in New Testament terms as threefold:

- Shalom proclaimed – kerygma.
- Shalom lived – Koinonia.
- Shalom demonstrated – diakonia.[45]

Raiser, one time leader of the World Council of Churches (WCC) would define it more in sociological terms, that is, working towards pluralism and economic development.[46] Newbigin's emphasis lies in the phrase the 'mission of Jesus', by which he means proclamation, expressed as Christocentric in his earlier, and Trinitarian in his later period.[47] He also describes mission as faith in action, love and hope in action, and action for God's justice.[48] For Jean Daniélou, mission is integrally bound up with spirituality:

> There is ... no opposition between contemplation and mission. The notion that there would be and that one would have to choose between them is absurd. On the contrary, mission appears as the self-unfolding of contemplation.[49]

Ad Gentes states:

> The mission of the Church is carried out by means of that activity through which in obedience to Christ's command and moved by the grace and love of the Holy Spirit, the Church makes itself fully present to all means and peoples in order to lead them to the faith, freedom and peace of Christ by the example of its life and teaching, by the sacraments and other means of grace.[50]

The presence of the Church, which shall be examined later in Newman's theology of mission, can be revealed in different ways. Bosch makes the point that whereas in the Celtic Church, pilgrimages

---

[45] Hoekendijk J. C. in Tijmes L. A. & P. (eds.) (1966) *The Church Inside Out*, trans. by W. L. Jenkins. London: SCM Press, p. 23.

[46] Raiser, K. (1991) *Ecumenism in Transition*, trans. by Tony Coates. Geneva: WCC Publications, pp. 31–53 and 79–111.

[47] See Goheen, M. W. (July 2002) 'As the Father has sent me, so I am sending you: Lesslie Newbigin's missionary ecclesiology' in *The International Review of Mission*, Vol. 91, No. 362, Geneva: WCC Publications. 355–367.

[48] Newbigin, L. (1995) *The Open Secret*. London: SPCK, pp. 32–65.

[49] Daniélou, J. (1996) *Prayer: The Mission of the Church*, trans. by D. L. Schindler. Edinburgh T&T Clark, p. 96.

[50] *The Documents of Vatican II:*, ed. by Abbott, W. H. (1966), London: Geoffrey Chapman, pp. 589ff.

became missions, in the Anglo Saxon Church, missionaries became church planters.[51]

Even though various definitions of mission are available, Bosch states that he still recognizes the elusiveness of defining something so grand as mission.[52] Yet an ecumenical statement *The Five Marks of Mission* has been adopted by a variety of churches. The marks are:

- To proclaim the good news of the Kingdom.
- To teach, baptize and nurture new believers.
- To respond to human need by loving service.
- To seek to transform the unjust structures of society.
- To strive to safeguard the integrity of creation and to sustain and renew the life of the earth.

This is not to say that mission is simple to define. As Bosch points out, it is elusive and Van der Water admits that when it comes to education for mission, the varying forms of education will make a difference to what counts as mission. For example, he cites Laurent Ramambason who regrets the ambiguous curriculum of missiology in popular courses and sees them often as lacking a holistic mission perspective.[53] In fact Andrew Wingate, one-time Principal of Queen's College Birmingham, who spent time in both England and India, noticed the difference in a short survey he carried out with his ministerial students in both countries. When asked what the students felt was most important in the curriculum, he noticed that in England the students placed pastoral studies foremost, then liturgical leadership, then preaching. Asking the same question of students in India, their responses were social service, challenging the unjust structures of society and interfaith encounters. He asked:

> What is mission? Is it methods of evangelism, or anything but evangelism? Is it a historical study, a study of missions or the reflection on a practical example

[51] Bosch, D. J. (1980) *Witness to the World*, London: Marshall, Morgan and Scott, p. 110.

[52] See Van der Water, D. P. (April 2005) 'Transforming theological education and ministerial formation', *The International Review of Mission*, Vol. 94, No. 373. Geneva: WCC Publications, p. 206.

[53] Van der Water, D. P. 'Transforming Theological Education and Ministerial Formation', pp. 206–207. Van der Water outlines three types of education, resulting in varying views of mission, namely paideia – education of the whole person, Wissenschaft – orderly disciplined research or professional education, and 'contextual education' courses, such as Theological Education by Extension (TEE), popular in some African, Asian and South American countries.

of mission, involving a placement? Is mission about presence or prophecy? And what is the place of cross-cultural mission? [54]

If he, as leader of an educational, theological community was asking these questions about the curriculum for mission in ministerial theological colleges, then clearly there are important questions for designers of these programmes, and at least the potential for confusion.

Highlighting this confusion about the definition of mission led two theologians to offer a major critique of mission in today's society in the West. Barrow and Smith's anthology, *Christian Mission in Western Society* is set within a dichotomy revealed in its first and last chapters. Smith paints Europe's religious landscape in a bleak fashion. In his view, people seem to have dispensed with Christian tradition which they feel is no longer true. By contrast Simon Barrow, at the end of the book, while agreeing that Christendom has had its age, sees the Church on the brink of waking up to new models of church with, 'a new kind of deliberately anti-exclusionary community founded on a rejection of violence, a costly embracing of the outsider, a local embracing of the global and a Christ-like willingness to stake their lives with those crucified "outside the gate" of our brave neo-liberal world'.[55]

ECCLESIOLOGY AND MISSION

There are three possible starting points for the present reformations of the Church in the West. The first is to address the decline in membership, second to address the reduced number of vocations to ordained leadership, third to attempt to lay foundations for a future shape of church. To begin by identifying a decline in membership of congregations, as many denominations are experiencing may very well lead to promoting a concern for mission. If this is the case then a clear definition of mission and its methodologies will be both helpful and motivating for those engaged in resolutions. Staring from noticing a reduced number of vocations to ordained leadership, as has happened in some denominations over the past fifty years, will

[54] Wingate, A. (April 2005) 'Overview of the history of the debate about theological education' in *The International Review of Mission*, Vol. 94, No. 373. Geneva: WCC Publications, p. 241.

[55] Barrow, S. and Smith, G. (2001) *Christian Mission in Western Society*. London: Churches Together in Britain, pp. 239–240.

likely result in the Church seeking to grow more leaders. In turn this will promote a debate over the function and responsibilities of leadership. Applied ministries, such as theologies of priesthood, laity and ministry will help direct training for leaders and will more likely encourage vocations to ordination from lay ministers. A third point of departure is to begin from the perspective of laying new foundations for the Church of the next generation. This will need to consider the consequent shape of the Church from actions made now. Like the parable of the sower and the seed, how the ground is prepared will have dramatic consequences for what is eventually successful and fruitful. This will be examined later and an example of such a new perspective is offered in Chapter 10. The contention here is that no matter where the starting point is, all three issues need to be given attention. They need to align to produce the most effective scenario of growth.

QUESTIONS:

- In what way does your church(es) understand and express the four *notes* – one, holy, catholic and apostolic?
- What are the faith statements that have shaped your church?
- What is the predominant view of mission in the church you serve?
- Of the *five marks of mission*, which does your church do best and which needs most improvement?

Chapter 3

GROWING THE PEOPLE OF GOD

LEADERSHIP, ECCLESIOLOGY AND CULTURE

What sort of leadership in the Church is needed if we take the Augustinian option seriously and face up the fact that are now living in a postmodern, post-Christian era but reject the sectarian option? While many will undoubtedly regard the Church's present situation as a serious loss, harking back to some supposedly golden age, e.g. to the Early Church before Constantine, to medieval Christendom, the Reformation or the Church before the Second Vatican Council, we must recognize that all ages of the Church have their ambiguities and nostalgia airbrushes out the contours that don't fit our ideal. Nevertheless, the past is something to be learnt from and may have riches which we rightly feel should be intelligently recovered. Not to know our past may mean mindlessly repeating our mistakes but can mean ignoring the wisdom as well.

Theologians have for centuries discussed what should be the attitude of the Church to the world in which it lives, to society and its values. We have to remember that the Church is not only in the world but the world is also present within it, which is why the Church is itself always in need of reform. In the last century much of this discussion was focused on the relationship between Christianity and culture. One of the most helpful contributions to this was Richard Niebuhr's book *Christ and Culture* in which he sets out five different positions that have been and can be adopted.[1] Each of these not only affects

---

[1] Niebuhr, H. Richard (1952) London, Faber and Faber. Note also Carter, Craig A. (2006) *Rethinking Christ and Culture*, Grand Rapids: Brazos Press for a critique and an alternative paradigm which raises the same questions about leadership.

our ecclesiology but also the view of what leadership in the Church should be trying to accomplish.

What did he mean by culture? Niebuhr suggests that culture should not be narrowly determined as that of a particular society or some aspect of it, e.g. science or philosophy, but it is about values – their realization and conservation – about human achievement although the latter should not be restricted to material goods but include all those aspects which go to make up what is seen as good for humanity and society. However culture is not uniform but has an inherent plurality about it, the product of human life and endeavour. Any description of this in the twenty-first century must take proper account of the many multicultural features of contemporary life. How will this affect what leadership in the Church must be for today?

Taking each of Niebuhr's positions in turn, we can see that they have implications for both ecclesiological emphasis and for leadership.

CHRIST AGAINST CULTURE

> Whatever may be the customs of the society in which the Christian lives, and whatever the human achievements it conserves, Christ is seen as opposed to them, so that he confronts men with the challenge of an 'either-or' decision.[2]

This is the language of the prophet, of proclamation and of conversion which stresses that the Gospel is radically different from any other system of values and that the Church should be trying to make it clear what the difference is. The hearer has to choose. Going out into society to communicate this effectively becomes a top priority here using all the means of communication now available. It comes nearest to what Dulles has described as the *Herald* image of the Church.[3] It is also most at home in the Exclusivist view of Christianity in relationship to other faiths. Little dialogue is possible with contemporary culture on this model. By itself it may not encourage leaders to listen or to see God at work in the world. It may be strong on teaching but may not promote genuine critical adult learning and may tend to support an authoritarian leadership style. While putting the response of faith in the forefront, a recognition that spirituality can exist outside the Church may be lacking. On the other hand the preparation for and support of adult Christian life as a witness will be

---

[2] Ibid. p. 54.
[3] Dulles, Avery (1974, 1987) *Models of the Church* (2nd edn) Gill and Macmillan, p. 76ff

fundamental to leadership aims. It is very pessimistic about human nature without grace and so has a very strong and focussed sense of mission and of discipleship, especially of the laity, and therefore can promote a real understanding of the content of belief.

CHRIST WITH CULTURE

A fundamental agreement between Christ and culture in which his:

> life and teachings are regarded as the greatest human achievement; it is in him, it is believed, the aspirations of men towards their values are brought to a point of culmination; he confirms what is best in the past and guides the process of civilization to its proper goal.[4]

Here we find a great emphasis on the humanity of Christ as someone to imitate. It looks for the best in contemporary culture in order to affirm it and will see the Church's role as working with the secular wherever possible, taking the world seriously. It is not authoritarian and indeed may tend to underplay the doctrinal aspects of the Gospel but will strongly emphasize service to the poor and the disadvantaged. It looks very much to secular, more democratic and accountable models of leadership, which could lead to an overemphasis on bureaucracy. On its own, it is not a model that encourages confrontational proclamation or prophetic witness, although it will stress advocacy of the disadvantaged. It comes nearest in Dulles' taxonomy to his model of the *Church as Servant*.[5] The sense of the spiritual and the transcendent may be less emphasized in favour of a more immanent sense of God and his truth being discoverable in the culture in which we are. Mission will be seen primarily as dialogue and thus there may be much less emphasis on inner spiritual renewal and conversion. This will focus an understanding of the Church's priorities in a rather different direction than Niebuhr's first category. There may be a tendency to see the work of the Church primarily in social work terms.

CHRIST ABOVE CULTURE

This affirms much of the second position but also argues that a great leap is required to bring society to a place which is beyond human achievement, i.e. 'a supernatural society and a new value centre'.[6]

---

[4] Ibid. p. 54.
[5] Ibid. p. 89ff.
[6] Ibid. p. 55.

This view, attributed to Aquinas, rests upon the theological premise that the role of the Church is to take humanity, damaged by sin, to its supernatural destination. Creation is affirmed as good, because of its Creator, but humanity's eyes need to be raised to the supernatural of which glimpses can be seen in creation itself but also in the liturgy, in art, and in the churches in which people worship. It recognizes the temptation that we have to view the material world as all there is and to be so absorbed in it as to be blind to our heavenly destiny. This promotes an alternative ideology which preachers like John Wesley and John Henry Newman denounced as leading to atheism. Like those chained up in Plato's Cave, eyes have to be opened so that the shackles of ignorance can be broken; grace needs to be accessed so that the pilgrim Christian can journey through life to the welcome that God has promised. It presents the Church with a vocation not just to support the individual but to bring about a spiritual ethos in society itself.

The danger of this view is to divinize the Church too much and therefore to gloss over the human tendencies of its members to succumb to the materialistic temptations of power, position and wealth disguised by pomp and circumstance. At its best it offers a different view of humanity, of society and of community. The place of worship becomes very important as a means of raising our eyes to heaven and refreshing the human spirit, although there is a danger of this becoming merely a musical performance. What it does stress is that all cultural expressions can become vehicles for the spiritual, for God encompasses the cosmos while affirming the different values by which Christians should live. It may, however, neglect the need for the prophetic, for proclamation, for challenge and the option for the poor. Dulles' models of the Church as *Mystical Communion* and as *Sacrament* belong here.[7] Leadership is not just about presiding at worship, important though that is. This model may need to be tempered also by the other idea of the Church as *People of God* with its sense, not just of the individual journey of each of us, but of the provisionality of the Church and its need to be open to uncertainty and change and to fresh forms and expressions. This is no abiding city. Leadership requires the maintenance of appropriate stability but also the capacity to lead in change which can be much more than simply trimming the boat.

---

[7] Ibid. Chapters 3 and 4.

CHRIST AND CULTURE IN POLAR TENSION

This takes both position 1 and position 2 together but accepts an inherent tension.

> Obedience to God requires obedience to the institutions of society and loyalty to its members as well as obedience to Christ who sits in judgment on that society. The resolution lies beyond history. Christians must endure this.[8]

This position goes back to Luther who, while sympathizing with the demands of the peasants in 1525 who were being very badly treated by the princes and also the Church, was prepared to tolerate tyranny on the grounds that opposition to the legal rulers of the state was not in accordance with the will of God. It was an issue that arose again when the churches considered what their response should be to the rise of Nazism in Germany. Some pastors like Dietrich Bonhoeffer made the decision to actively oppose Hitler but some have argued that the position adopted by Luther left the Church uncertain as to what to do under tyranny. Luther recognized the tension that his position created but in effect seemed to be proposing two moralities; a spiritual or personal morality, and a public, secular one.

This position tends to privatize religion and therefore make a separate domain for personal faith as distinct from secular life. There are advocates of this among Christians but it is also the view of secularists. Faith is to be tolerated provided that it does not obtrude upon anyone else. It would not be a position that the political theologians, especially the Liberation Theologians, would adopt since they denied that it is possible to separate public and private in this way for this is to misunderstand the very heart of the Gospel. Nevertheless, it represents a real problem that the Church has to address: how should Christians manifest their belief in their secular contexts. How political should the Church be? At what point, if any, must the *Servant* model of church be replaced by the *Herald* one? Must any genuine spirituality have social consequences not just by promoting spiritual health but by an opposition to what Liberation Theology would call 'structural sin'? Do we have to accept that we live by two moralities and endorse that? Where is discipleship to be exercised on this view? This runs the risk of so emphasizing the transcendent nature of religion as to neglect social justice and critical engagement with the world on the grounds that resolution of this tension can and should be left to God. It may lead also to the Church becoming Erastian

[8] Ibid. p. 55.

functioning uncritically as the religious arm of the state. This can be a particular problem in countries (mainly in Europe) where there are close links between church and state. Paradoxically, it has been noted by sociologists like Grace Davie, that it is in these countries that hostility to religion is being most expressed.[9] Is this because the Church and its leadership are regarded as hopelessly compromised?

CHRIST AS THE CONVERTER OF MAN IN HIS CULTURE AND SOCIETY

In this position the potential and actual opposition of the Gospel and society is recognized but this is not just to be endured as the previous position might suggest. It is a converging approach in society that may take a very long time.[10]

This last position, Niebuhr suggests, is associated with both Calvin and St Augustine but claims that it is the duty of the Church to work for the conversion of society to the Gospel, using all the means available. Calvin clearly envisages a Christian state, but St Augustine takes a more eschatological view and is, arguably, more pessimistic about its realization and realistic about the kind of struggle Christians will need to be engaged in. Newman puts the problem typically when he wrote, that left to themselves people tend:

> To settle down in a satisfied way in the world as they find it, to sit down in the 'mire and dirt' of their natural state, to immerse themselves and be absorbed in the unhealthy marsh which is under them. They tend to become part of the world, and be sucked in by it, and (as it were) changed into it; and to lose all aspirations and thoughts, whether good or bad after anything higher than what they are.[11]

This view, however, is not dissimilar to the view of Aquinas of raising society up to a supernatural plane and that therefore the role of the Church, like the spire of a great cathedral, is to make humans aspire to what is beyond their own nature, but this view presupposes Christendom which arguably is now no more and whose assumptions now do not underpin society and culture. So what happens when the Church is in a situation of competing ideologies within a culture? It is here that the Augustinian view may be more realistic, for society is

---

[9] Davie, Grace (2002) *Europe: The Exceptional Case, Parameters of Faith in the Modern World.* London: DLT.

[10] Ibid. p. 56.

[11] Newman, J. H. *Parochial and Plain Sermons.* Vol. IV, p. 162.

then a place where the Christian voice struggles to be heard so that leadership involves keeping up hope and trust in the way ahead.

Three things need to be stressed at this stage of the discussion: the first is the importance of being a people of faith and hope in a God who keeps His Covenant; the second is that, like the People of Israel at the Exodus, we must learn to live with uncertainty for, like the sands of the desert, the contours will change frequently; the third is that loss can also be gain in that we have a freedom to slough off some of the burdens of the past and to discover new ways of being the Church, that are faithful to our roots but open to the future. God may want it done differently.

If the Church has lost or is losing much of its position, power and influence, images and metaphors like *soul, salt, leaven* or *seed* may have more life in them then more traditional ones suggesting that the way forward will be more about being a presence *within* society, in dialogue with it and about persuasion rather than command. The Church may need to learn to be a Socratic partner, enabling as well as challenging, learning as well as teaching, reflecting as well as questioning, offering rather than imposing, modelling new forms of living rather than demanding them. A rightly communicated apologetic may be one of the key tasks of leadership here for which we need Augustinian wisdom.

St Augustine, however, was not just the advocate of the long haul. In his *City of God* he reflects upon two kinds of love which characterize the earthly city and the heavenly city and the need to discern where they may coincide and where, essentially they differ.[12] Both cities are concerned with law and order and on this they can find agreement, but on heavenly matters there can and must be dissent and difference. It will be here that true religion comes under attack. What St Augustine is advocating here is the need for discernment, for insight that must surely be cultivated by any religious leader. What is of the Gospel and what is not? Religious faith is always in tension precisely because it seek to raise human living towards an ideal towards which the earthly city can be an ally but also its implacable enemy. The sectarian option tries to deal with the problem by withdrawal, its opposite by capitulation. The Christian always has to face the possibility that the Gospel *salt* will not bring improvement and that the *bread* may not rise or that it will be cast out.

What are we seeking to do when we try to be *salt* or *leaven* to society as distinct from the change of heart that is addressed to individuals?

---

[12] Book XIV, Chapter xxviii.

The connection between the Gospel and justice must be central to this but it is wider than that. St Augustine discusses this under the theme of peace which everyone desires but which many mistakenly locate in the wrong things. For him peace is a universal order or law emanating from God and pervading all creation. There are various kind of peace, he says: peace of the body, of the soul and of the body and soul. There is a peace between an individual and God, and peace between two people. Then there is peace of a household and of the state in which citizens live in rule and obedience. Lastly, there is the peace of the *City of God* which is an ordered and harmonious companionship in enjoying God and one another in God.

This suggests that the Church should be seeking in itself as well as in the world to realize that sense of peace which God has ordained and to which humans aspire but often fall short of or mistake for something else. It is clear not only is the main means to the love of God, our neighbour and ourselves, but also that those who are in positions of authority should exercise that as servants, ruling not with ambition or proud sovereignty but in love and mercy.[13] What is required is the establishment of an order of things based on faith and a perception of what true peace based on right relations means.

For this to happen, then church leadership in the twenty-first century cannot be simply about inviting people into the Church to be nourished and taught but about forming a community of discernment, perception and courage which looks outwards towards the society in which they live and bringing a spirit of leavening to fruition. Traditionally, this is the language of martyrdom. The words of dismissal at the end of the Eucharist are meant to do precisely that, having first led people through a ritual of acknowledgement of times of failure, forgiveness, reconnection with the Gospel, rededication and offering, spiritual nourishment and strengthening as they take up again the pilgrim journey. This has to be based on a sense of community support and the knowledge that they do not walk alone. Leadership here has to be also about community building that gives people courage to go out rather than a refuge from danger, although that will have its place.

In what ways, if any, might Christian leadership be compared to that in other walks of life? How might it be different? If the Church imitated secular models more, would it commend itself to people more effectively? There is some evidence that this is where some

---

[13] Book XIV, Chapter xiv.

commentators would have the Church go and the language used seems to express this; clergy effectiveness needs to be measured, some would say, in ways similar to other professions so that appropriate standards can be ensured. Leaders need to develop competences and there need to be benchmarks to assess these. While it may be true that some of the Church's problems have arisen because its leaders did not always behave in professional ways when they should have done, there is a danger of making the ordained leadership, at least, into something alien to what the Church is. In that sense, the Church is and has to be countercultural.

During the consultation period before the appointment of a new Archbishop of Westminster in 2008, several prominent theologians and public figures were asked what qualities they hoped the new archbishop might have. Predictably there was some divergence of view but one person said that it should be 'someone who does not want the job'. There are good biblical and historical precedents for this as some of the most successful leaders of the People of Israel and the Christian Church have taken up their task with considerable reluctance and personal misgivings whereas by contrast some of the most disastrous leaders have been consumed with personal ambition and self-importance. Yahweh warns the people through Samuel of the dangers of kingship (1 Sam. 8.10ff) and Jesus, too, tells his disciples that their leadership must be about being a servant and that they must avoid the kind of leadership prevalent in the Gentile world (Mark 10.42-45).

The Church has always struggled with this and the temptations of power and affluence, particularly if it is both in the world but yet not of it, as it strives to be. Most of its structures and bureaucratic procedures are similar to those of any secular organization and have to be if it is to function fairly, efficiently and in accordance with law. As Stephen Sykes has pointed out, the Church has a role to play in society as an institution and therefore the same temptations to abuse power and fail to use it properly exist as in any secular organization.[14] He cites the example of Pope Gregory the Great as the reluctant leader who wrote one of the most important handbooks about Episcopal leadership, the *Regula Pastoralis* which, he claims, has still much to teach us about the dangers of high office in the Church, or for that matter, anywhere.[15] But the Church's calling is

---

[14] Sykes, Stephen (2006) *Power and Christian Theology*. Continuum.
[15] Ibid. pp. 138ff.

to bring the Gospel to humankind and to be an effective sign of the Kingdom of God. Leaders in the Church must and do exercise power and authority but how they do so and for what purpose become the crucial question and a crucial means of proclamation of the Gospel. The purpose of the Church and what makes it different is that corporately it is concerned with the deepest meaning of human life and it represents this by what it is as well as by what it does. It is a sermon expressed not just in stones but in people and how they are brought together. This must mean that this symbolic character accrues not just to the Church as a body of people but also to certain kinds of leadership within it as well.

The question of whether leadership in the Church is different from secular organizations thus cannot be answered without reference to what the Church is and how it conceives of its purpose, in other words to ecclesiology, as was emphasized in the last chapter. That there are different ecclesiologies within the Christian Church is readily apparent to any student of Church History although today this needs to be tempered by the many signs of convergence in ecumenical documents of the last century or so. While being mindful of the differences, this discussion will concentrate on where there seems to be some common ground. One crucial question that needs to be noted is whether the ordained role is conceived of primarily as 'ontological' or as 'functional', i.e. between what a person has *become* as a result of ordination and what a person now has the authority to *do*. This will be explored in depth in a later chapter but it may suffice to note here that perhaps the differences might not be as great as might first be presupposed and that some parallels can be drawn with secular models of leadership.

TWO LANGUAGES?

One major problem in trying to draw parallels and distinctions between an ecclesiologically-based understanding of leadership and that derived from the social sciences is that of comparing two very different kinds of language, although it is interesting to note how secular organizations have adopted a theological word *mission* into their vocabulary. Clergy are often resistant to importing the language of the social sciences into their discourse about leadership on the grounds that the Church is not a secular organization and should not be described as such nor should the theological terms simply be translated into those used by contemporary organizational theory. These languages can be described as *fiduciary*, i.e. making use of images and metaphors on the one hand and analytical or management English on the other.[16] An attempt will be made to bring these two languages closer together.

When religious discourse makes extensive use of language which is 'analogical, metaphorical or symbolic' we respond by 'acting out the claims they make'.[17] In other words, religion uses ritual and primarily poetic means of expression, e.g. hymns and liturgy to convey and involve people in what it is about. This form of language has been called 'fiduciary' because it is taken on trust to inform our whole lives and put us in touch with what is deeply meaningful. It engages not just the mind but our emotions and often requires a response before we reflect upon it. The ordination services of the different Christian Churches make extensive use of such language to indicate what the role is and accompany this by ritual acts which symbolize it, i.e. by what is called a *performance utterance.*

Images speak to us more profoundly and at a deeper level than other forms of communication; they have a kind of sacramental character about them, pointing to a reality which lies beneath and beyond what is said or portrayed and can inspire us time and time again, revealing yet more of itself.

We can understand some things when we find out that we can express them in another way or equally well in our own words. This is the way of explanation and of description in which there are alternative words or ways of saying something. However, some things are better grasped because the words and images are right and in the right order. This is the way of the Bible, of drama, poetry and of art. A poem, a play or a hymn is great because it is resistant to paraphrase and is convertible. No other words will do. To understand the Gospel means engaging with and entering into the images and stories of Scripture rather like we understand a Shakespearean play by attending a performance and being drawn into it as well as by discussing it critically afterwards. Biblical criticism needs to be balanced by a devotional and *fiduciary* apprehension of Scripture as a living and symbolic reality if the riches of our heritage are to continue to inspire us. We have trust in these images and ways of speaking because we experience them as life-giving.

[16] Cf Coulson, John (1981) *Imagination and Belief.* Oxford: Clarendon Press pp. 14ff.

[17] Coulson, John (1970) *Newman and the Common Tradition.* Oxford: Clarendon Press, p. 4.

In a similar way, we know what the Church is through participating in its liturgy and its imagery as well as by reflecting on its life and practice and comparing it to other bodies we have experienced. It is understood by entering into it, as well as something that can be known objectively or scientifically. The Church is thus both an organization capable of being expressed and re-expressed in different words, like any other but also an image engaging us emotionally as well as intellectually at the deepest point of our being, for it is, despite its human imperfections, a living symbol and therefore irreducible. That is how it speaks or should do, if we will let it. How else, too, are we to understand those paradoxical words of Jesus in Mark 10.45 or the images of vine and branches, of leaven and salt? A true symbol always partakes of the reality it renders intelligible[18] and thus has life within it. The more you re-visit it, the greater is the depth of perception.

The opposite of fiduciary language is *analytic* language which is meant to be simple, literal, descriptive objective and empirical, requiring little use of imagery and appealing primarily to the understanding rather than the emotions. It is much more like everyday language. Coulson notes in his extensive discussion of this topic that it was the language favoured by the Utilitarians of whom many were deeply suspicious of poetry, regarding it as a form of misrepresentation.[19] What on earth can it mean, for example, to refer to an ordained person as a *shepherd* or to Christ as the *Lamb of God* or the Church as the *Body of Christ* if analytical language is to be preferred? How can we bring these two kinds of discourse together in any kind of meaningful way in talking about leadership? Failure to do so is to perpetuate an unhelpful divide and mutual suspicion. The widespread use of logos today is an indication that secular organizations, too, need ways of expressing what they are about other than *plain* language, but we need *plain* language as well to answer the question 'yes, but what does it mean in practice?'. Fiduciary language consists of the images and narratives that are the wellsprings of any tradition, the founding story which tells us who we are. To use them and to re-visit them is a form of *anamnesis* bringing the past into the present in order to direct our future. To situate leadership within these is critically important not to replicate the past but to grow from it authentically to the future. This theme will be developed further in a later chapter.

---

[18] I am indebted for these insights to John Coulson's *Imagination and Belief*, pp. 14ff.
[19] Coulson ibid. pp. 6–7.

WHAT IS LEADERSHIP?

Is leadership of the Church, especially by the ordained person, essentially different from that of the secular world? The answer is yes and no which is why any study of it must be firmly grounded in theology as well as insights from other sources in the founding narratives, because good leadership of whatever kind should be profoundly creative and moral. Some important secular descriptions provided by Paul Avis[20] will prove to be helpful first of all:

> A leader shapes and shares a vision which gives point to the work of others (Handy).[21]

> The key task of leadership is to define the institution's mission and role creatively; to relate it to internal and external factors; to embody it in the social structure of the institution so that it shapes its character (Selznick).[22]

Leadership of any organization embodies something which is communicated to others in a way that makes membership meaningful and its existence intelligible. It is grounded in an understanding of reality both within the institution and outside it and it is this which enables the organization to have an appropriate shape and form to accomplish appropriately what it was set up to do. The key words here are: 'shape' and 'share', 'define creatively',' relate to the internal and the external', and 'embody'. Was this not what the Exodus story was about? The Covenant with God and the promise that came with it together with the way of life that Moses communicates to the people gave point to the arduous, often dispiriting Exodus journey. Left to themselves the people often strayed from the vision and were tempted to worship a god they could make for themselves (Exod. 32). Even Aaron had lost sight of the vision and had let the people *run wild* (Exod. 32.25). A very human story, which as it continues, has Moses unfolding the purposes of God to the people of Israel, shaping their lives, discovering their identity, for they have been commanded not to imitate the way of life of those among whom they will live, but to live faithfully as God has commanded them (Deut. 18.9ff). God promises to raise up a prophet to remind and recall the people to their covenant relationship (Deut. 18.15).

[20] Avis, Paul (1992) *Authority, Leadership and Conflict in the Church. London:* Mowbray pp. 107ff for these and further examples.

[21] Handy, Charles (1989) *The Age on Unreason.* London: Business Books. p. 106.

[22] Selznick, P. (1966) *Leadership in Administration: A Sociological Interpretation.* New York: Harper.

Although both the quotations from Handy and Selznick might be primarily applicable to an organization with a product to sell, they are, in fact, equally applicable to what can be described as service industries, eg the health service or various forms of social welfare. The most important task of leadership is to facilitate the shaping of a clear vision and purpose because it is this that helps people to make sense of their work for the organization. In many ways, one of the problems of churches is that most people see themselves as passive recipients or clients rather than as contributors or co-workers. The emphasis on collaborative styles of working adopted by the Christian churches in recent years tries to see members as both client and co-worker, responsible for and to each other. The increasing emphasis on an active laity with a vocation as a Christian, rather than a purely passive one who comes to receive pastoral care, has implications for how leadership works with the membership to shape a vision and communicate it. We need to move from dependency to interdependency. The leadership has not only to articulate the mission of the Church but also to relate this both to the founding story and to the context in which it is, so that it shapes the Church in the here and now, rather than simply perpetuating an anachronistic model. This has implications for leadership in change, perhaps the greatest challenge facing any leader. The lesson of the Exodus story and of the history of Israel is that there need to be people who exercise the prophetic charism within any organization and especially the Church that reminds us of the founding vision and story. The liturgy of course does this, but we still need the challenging voice of the prophet.

Of course the Church does not have a mission that can be described adequately in the measurable terms that would now be used by most secular institutions and so needs the fiduciary or symbolic kind of language which points beyond itself, embodying the narrative. Here the task of a theology of the Church is to inform our understanding of the leadership role. The temptation of a tradition which sees itself in purely bureaucratic terms is that it will all the time be reducing fiduciary language to management or analytic language.

Nevertheless it is surely right to say that:

> The penalty for failure to define the primary task, vision or mission of an institution is confusion in the organisation, blurring of its values and inability to evaluate task performance.[23]

---

[23] Rice, A. K. (1963) *The Enterprise and its Environment*. London: Tavistock p. 190.

If the leadership does not clearly delineate and communicate what the primary task or mission is, then everyone will be confused as to what they are about and what they stand for. There will also be no criteria whereby people know that they are doing the right thing or doing it right. This can only lead to failure. Put in theological terms, if the Church does not know its story, does not trust is basic images, has no means of testing authenticity, is unaware of its theological DNA so to speak, then it too will not know what it is about. How far might the decline of the Christian Church in Western Europe be due to this kind of muddle? To answer this question requires the kind of analysis pioneered by Niebuhr and Dulles, in which the question that has to be answered is what does the Gospel demand of us in relationship to the world? What biblical and other images will energize us in the context in which we now are? How do we read the signs of the times theologically? What parts of the founding story do we need to re-visit and allow to speak to us?

LEADERS AS TRUSTEES

Leadership in the Church, then, requires a sense of accountability to the sources of the vision which he or she is called to shape and share as well as to the context in which a church finds itself. This is a kind of developmental dialogue and reflective practice which is consequent on being *in the world but not of it* and can be called *accountability to the vision* to distinguish it from the *accountability of procedures*. It will be particularly visible when leading change and is best expressed as a series of reflective questions which try to assess that a church really is earthed in its context but is also being true to the sources of its vision and mission. The questions also seek to discover how far there is a gap between the theology and vision we profess (accepted theology) and the actual theology that we act out (theology-in-practice).[24] A model for this will be explored in Chapter 4.

This is a form of accountability that can be called *trusteeship of the vision* which demands constant vigilance. Is this an apostolic role in which case where is it to be found?

It will be noticed that on this model, derived from reflective practice, the vision is not something static but organic and is at least as much to do with *doing the right thing* as with *doing it right*. What will be the right thing is dependent upon a number of variables and the

[24] Adapted from Schön, Donald (1996) *The Reflective Practitioner*. Aldershot: Ashgate.

wells of wisdom that are sought out and *visited*. The exercise will be cyclic and ongoing as a church community reflects on the ways in which it is trying to be faithful to the Gospel.

For example, Scripture provides stories and images handed down, interpreted and added to through past generations which show how varied leadership can be and the need to exercise it as trustees of the vision; 1 Corinthians 12 tells us of the variety of spiritual gifts that God has given the Church to be used for His purposes, for there are varieties of gifts, services, activities and manifestations of the Spirit for *the common good* (1 Cor. 12.4ff). Apostles and deacons become the basis for other ministries in Acts 6.1-7 and there is group ministry at Antioch led by the Spirit in Acts 13.1-3 from whom Barnabas and Saul are drawn for a specific work. A division of labour is made according to gifts under the headship of Christ in Ephesians 4.1-16 to 'equip the saints for the work of ministry, for building up the body of Christ' (Eph. 4.12). The scholarly Ezra explains the Law to the people and interprets it with Nehemiah and the Levites. They 'gave the sense, so that the people understood' (Neh. 8). Priests are set aside for a permanent liturgical ministry in Exodus 29 and there is a delegation of the burden of authority and ministry in Exodus 18 who will 'bear the burden' with Moses (Exod. 18.22).

If one of the roles of a pastor is to enable all to find their place, then another must be to help them grow as adult Christians in their understanding of their vocation and in their sense of responsibility for the work and mission of the Church. This is not something that has to be done because in many parts of the world, there is a shortage of clergy, but rather it needs to be done in order to be the Church.

None of the examples can simply be translated into management English, but there is overlap, because these accounts tell us what the role is, not just what it does or is for. What we notice from these texts is the importance of working as 'knitted together by every ligament with which it is equipped' (Eph. 4:16) and Jesus' warnings about the temptations of status (Mk 9.33 and 10.35) which show how the disciples struggled to really understand what the Gospel (the vision) was about. Belonging in this way is, therefore, part of the Gospel sign which not only portrays it to those outside the Church but also reminds the community itself of what it is or should be. It also tells us that leadership is rarely effective if it is exercised alone which is why most churches today are trying to stress the importance of collaborative ministry.

For collaborative ministry to work, however, there has to be a different style of leadership than the autocratic *do it all, lone ranger* model of the past centuries which, in any case, has no basis in the New Testament or the very Early Church or in more recent ecclesiological documents, although seemingly endemic in many congregations.[25] Such a style encourages lay passivity 'you're the priest/pastor/ minister, you do it' rather than 'how can we do it together?' Proper stress needs to be placed, therefore, on how each congregation, which may be part of a cluster of churches, can be formed in collaborative ministry in its locale. This demands a change of culture and ethos from dependency to interdependency and that, of course will take time. It is also countercultural in terms of the individualism of our own time. The lead has to be given by those who are called to the ordained roles.

These considerations mean that any form of leadership, whether in the Church or in secular life, needs to have people who can see the big picture and who are in touch with the underlying culture. One writer put it: 'Other people can cope with the waves; it is the leader's job to watch the tide'.[26] It is all too tempting as an ordained person to be so caught up with the minutiae of church organization that he or she fails to discern the signs of the times, the general trend of things, and thus not to see the whole as well as the parts, e.g.:

- How is the climate changing in this community?
- What are its overall concerns?
- What is being done well and what could be improved?
- Is this still a dependency culture or is it one that is learning to be interdependent?
- Is the community growing adult Christians and if so, what is the difference that is making the difference?

All these are questions that are different from the day-to-day management ones that are about coping with the next day, the next week, the next month, but not with the question of 'what course or direction are we taking?' or 'what kind of people have we become?'. Too much exercise of leadership is really simply a form of management doing it right but avoiding the question 'are we doing the right thing?' and 'are we communicating to people what the right thing is?'.

Many of these leadership questions are really theological or philosophical questions which tend to get marginalized, especially in a

---

[25] E.g. *Lumen Gentium* and *Called to Love and Praise.*
[26] Jay, A. (1967) *Management and Machiavelli.* London: Hodder p. 139.

society which is obsessed with measurable outcomes and targets. In the educational world of the twenty-first century, schools and colleges and universities are inundated with measurable targets but arguably have little time to ask whether the targets set are worth meeting. The Church needs to avoid this trap, because it is concerned with setting before people a vision of life, a whole way of understanding ourselves, the world and the cosmos that is theocentric. The patristic adage 'Christ became what we are so that we might become what He is' is one metaphor for expressing the vision that the Gospel brings. Communicating this well is what attracts people, for commitment to it cannot be coerced. It is a covenant relationship that makes sometimes difficult journeys not only bearable but actually possible, as the people of Israel discovered, overcoming doubt, loss of hope and of faith. Good leadership empowers, strengthens, motivates, lifting people to heights they never dreamt possible, making the future more than a dream, but a reality.

SPIRITUAL LEADERSHIP

Traditionally Christian leadership, especially of the ordained has been described as *spiritual*. Frequently, what this has been interpreted to mean is that leaders in the Church are concerned with the private, sacral, individual and hidden aspects of human living and that they and the Church itself have no place in the public square or are simply other worldly. Indeed the secularizing trends of contemporary society seem to demand this. In effect Christianity is expected to become a sect and increasingly to vacate the stage of public life. The consequence of this is that other value systems take its place. It is the argument of this book that not only does this misconstrue the term *spiritual* but it also is a mistaken view of the place and role of the Church. It reinforces the view that what happens in church or in a house group is divorced from what happens in the work place or in ordinary life, leading in effect to two moralities or modes of existence.

There are three meanings to the word *spiritual* which are relevant to our theme. The first is that it is the mission of the Church to bring the insights and spirit of the Gospel to all aspects of human living whether public or private and it will be one of the principal roles of the leadership of the Church to facilitate this, for the Church is an agent of change for all human activity. Second, the Church sees all areas of human life in a dimension as parts to a whole of a

God-bearing cosmos and this is something that needs to be enacted and communicated. The third meaning of the term implies that the leadership of the Church can only enable people to do this if they themselves are striving to be animated and imbued by the spirit of the Gospel, trying to become closer to the triune God and to share this with others, from the living source of their faith. The life of prayer, of contemplation, of devotion and worship is thus of supreme importance.

The symbolic ritual which speaks of all this is the Eucharist. At this the community, lay and ordained, leaders and led, come together from their ordinary lives to confess, make peace and ask for God's help, to receive the Word, to proclaim their faith, to offer themselves and their gifts, be refreshed from the Lord's table so that they may go forth strengthened once more to 'love and serve the Lord' with God's blessing upon them. It is an image of transformation and integration whose purpose is to sanctify the world. This is the spirituality of *salt* or *leaven*, of being an agent of change by being authentically what God wants each Christian to be. Because of human frailty, this will always be an aspiration rather than a full realization, which is why the structure of the Eucharist reminding us that we need forgiveness and refreshment is so important. This aspect of leadership is thus about modelling this and by doing so to animate others to be agents of transformation also.

The vision provided by the Gospel is of what the whole of human life could be like if it is lived in Christ. It is a value system and a perspective which challenges all others and it is only by constant reference to it that sense can be made of any plans or strategies which a local church community may make. The task of leadership here is both to hold up this vision before the eyes of the people but also to motivate them to believe that it can be made a reality and thus to shape ways in which all can be engaged in this task not just through important projects or schemes but in the living of ordinary life. Above all, the task is to enable people to live in the world and to play their full part in it, but yet be not of it in terms of their values and perspectives and to live with this tension in faith and hope. This is the Augustinian option.

In the aftermath of the scandals revealed in the Catholic Church in Ireland, many commentators spoke of the need to be a more open and humble church, recalling Jesus' teaching about power in the Gospels, notably Mark 10.45. Hill quotes St Augustine's sermon 23 to illustrate this:

> For although to all appearances I am standing in a higher place than you, this is merely for the convenience of carrying my voice better, and in fact it is you who are in the higher place to pass judgment, and I who am being judged. We bishops are called teachers, but in many matters we seek a teacher ourselves, and we certainly don't want to be regarded as masters ... the office of master is dangerous, the state of disciple safe.[27]

This was echoed by Cardinal Suenens when he wrote: 'A true leader, ultimately responsible for the pastoral work of the locale, will find his place when he has succeeded in helping others find theirs'.[28]

Finding your place in the world, in the Church, in your family is a useful metaphor for the human journey not in the sense of being *put in your place* by others in power positions but in terms of finding out where you can belong. The idea of the Christian leader having *no place* until he or she has found a place for everyone else is one interpretation of servant leadership. In fact churches are often laid out so that the only people who have a definite place are the clergy and those performing liturgical service. Laypeople may be very jealous of *their* place in the Church literally or metaphorically. Who has a *place* in this church and who does not may be an important test of its inclusivity, its theology and understanding of Christian leadership and ministry. The Christ who reached out to those on the margins, without 'a place' must thus become the exemplar of leadership in the Church.

QUESTIONS

- How do you understand the term church? What view of leadership best fits with that?
- How helpful is it to talk about Christian leadership in terms of measurable skills and competences?
- Do the secular quotations about leadership throw light on what is often missing about the Church and its mission or do they miss the point?
- What issues are there about power in the Church today?
- Does there need to be exclusivity as well as inclusivity in the Church?

[27] Sermon 23 translated by Hill, Edmund OP (1988), in *Ministry and Authority in the Catholic Church.* London: Chapman p. 76.
[28] Suenens, L. (1968) *Co-responsibility in the Church.* London: Burns and Oates p. 58.

Chapter 4

FOUNDATIONAL ROLES IN THE CHURCH

Many people find the language that the Church uses about itself confusing and unclear. This is not just because there are different ecclesiologies, which may be at variance with each other, but also because it seems that some terms are used without a great deal of precision. Furthermore, the increasing use of the laity to engage in the Church's work rather than simply be the recipient of it, raises the question of what may be the difference, if any between an ordained person and the laity. Some traditions have an ecclesiology which in effect says there is no difference, others that there is an essential difference between lay and ordained, although it is difficult sometimes to discover in what the difference consists. The language of *Priest, Presbyter* and *Minister* often seems to regard the terms as interchangeable, although each tradition has their own understanding of them usually depending on whether the role is understood ontologically or functionally. It then becomes difficult to be clear as to what kind of leadership they are expected to exercise, especially when a more active laity is being encouraged to develop. No longer is the omnicompetent practitioner who *does it all* the desirable model for which people are trained for they must learn to work with others. This means changing the language and some of the ritual. Even in the non-conformist traditions, which tend to see ordination or authorization in functional terms, the term *The Minister* is reserved for the ordained person: 'You're the minister, you do it.' In induction services the service seems to emphasize where ministry lies by particular rituals which stress the exclusive responsibilities of the incumbent.

John Tiller in a seminal book written with Mark Birchall illustrates the problem very well.[1] A group of clergy were called together

---

[1] Tiller, John with Birchall, Mark (1987) *The Gospel Community and its Leadership.* Basingstoke: Marshall-Pickering pp. 128ff.

to devise a vocational leaflet entitled *Wanted: Leaders in Tomorrow's Church*. After a good deal of discussion the group identified five broad areas of leadership: worship; vision forming; pastor and spiritual guide; prophet, evangelist and teacher; and lastly, administrator. They soon realized that while all these were areas that needed to be done, few people, if any, had either the gifts or the time to do them all. The position is transformed, however, Tiller argues, if leadership is seen as corporate and shared, i.e. as a team, but it is important to develop that idea further by suggesting that the work of a church is the responsibility of everyone albeit in different ways, not just those who have particular authorized roles and that this should be our starting point.

The model offered here is an attempt to clarify the language, bringing together insights from secular views of leadership and management with theological images and metaphors. Its starting point is what is usually referred to as *the priesthood of all believers* or, *the priesthood of all the baptized*, i.e. what all Christians have in common. This avoids the common mistake of the past which was to treat the *real* church as those who are ordained with the laity regarded as a passive add-on. Such an approach emphasizes that all have a vocation as members of the Church and therefore a part to play in its mission, rather than seeing vocation as something which belongs exclusively to those who are ordained or officially authorized, for this is to clericalize all ministry. Any discussion of leadership must thus be based on a sound ecclesiology which does justice to all the members.

This means replacing a *pyramid* model (Figure 4:1) of church with something different.

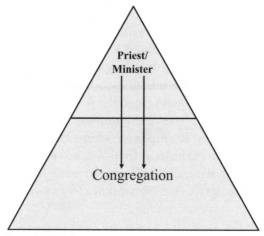

Figure 4:1 The Pyramid Model

The problem with the pyramid model, which the Church seems largely to have adopted, even after the Reformation, is the assumption that ordained or authorized persons are omnicompetent, which is not true to experience. It also tends to produce passive laity which receives rather than gives or shares. Communication is largely one-way and of the 'I tell, you do' variety. It tends also to clericalize all ministry or service and sees the ordained or authorized person as someone who is apart from the congregation that he or she seeks to serve. While it is possible to flatten the pyramid somewhat and to expand the upper section into a ministry team, this does not really do justice to the *priesthood of all believers* concept. The pyramid model tends also to perpetuate a dependency and more autocratic way of being the Church which deskills everybody. The ordained can be kept firmly in their place and the congregation in theirs which may suit both sides as a way of resisting the growth of adult ways of being a Christian. Congregations are also inclined to always be looking for the ideal priest or minister who is omnicompetent and who, of course, does not exist which absolves them from playing their full part as members of the Church. In effect, the pyramid model is *mission impossible* even though attractive in hierarchically structured churches.

It may be tempting to think that very bureaucratic models of church get over the pyramid problem but they can be hierarchical also. Committees resourced by an inner core can be very effective at ensuring that nothing gets done as well as providing a helpful forum for debate and ideas. The pyramid divide can take many forms.

The important point to note here is that the pyramid model actually prevents the ordained from exercising their role as fully as they might, first because they cannot play to their strengths, and second because they have expectations heaped upon them that are unrealistic. What is even more important is that it is based on a theology, which does not acknowledge the teaching of the New Testament of the ways in which God has distributed gifts and charisms among the people in ways which are mutually complementary. To say that one person cannot have all the strengths and gifts to fulfil what the Church requires for its work and mission is not a weakness, as the pyramid model really suggests (and therefore you try ever harder to compensate for that or just give up) but actually a recognition that we need each other. This will be explored further when we consider team working.

The situation becomes even clearer when churches have to be clustered in some way because of a shortage of clerical personnel or because of economics or dwindling congregations:

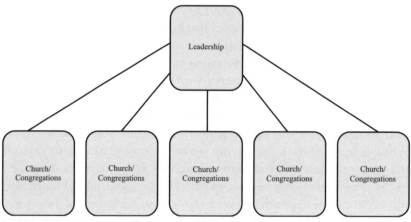

Figure 4:2 Leadership

On this model (Figure 4:2), the leadership has to simply add on other units of worship and be the *do-it-all* minister for each. This, of course leads to work overload and consequently to minimal pastoral or mission activity. If the leadership then insists on fulfilling their role as they would if they had only one church or congregation to look after, then, like the hamster in its treadmill, they either have to peddle faster and faster until exhaustion sets in or do it differently. However, the argument of this chapter is that they need to be doing it differently anyway based upon a better ecclesiology which values the vocation of every member of the People of God and a theology of the role of the ordained person which frees them to fulfil their calling.

In Figure 4:3 the tambourine itself is meant to represent the congregation with smaller circles representing the different foci of Gospel witness and work in which they participate. The circles are on the borders of the larger circle to suggest that all Gospel work and witness looks both outwards and inwards. Following Suenens, the leadership in an important sense has 'no place' in that its role is to resource and underpin the vocation of all, helping each person to find 'their place' in Gospel witness and work. The leadership can therefore be free, as needed, to be either for a time *in* some of the smaller circles, or at the centre of the large circle or outside the structure altogether having helped to equip each part for Gospel service. Where the ordained leadership is located at any time becomes thus an issue of priorities, need and strategy rather than *gap-filling* or trying to do it all.

The tambourine could equally well represent a cluster of congregations in which each needs to be largely equipped for its own Gospel witness and work. This does not make the ordained leadership less

The mission and work of the Church in this locale.

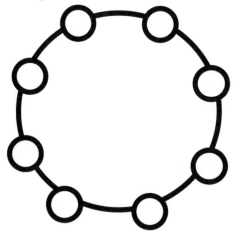

*The circles represent areas of the Church's work and mission, e.g. evangelism,
liturgy, social outreach.*

Figure 4:3 The 'Tambourine'

important but rather, on the contrary, emphasizes its enabling and
symbolic character.

MINISTRY

Traditionally the Gospel witness and work has been referred to by
the term 'ministry'. Today it is a word that has some unfortunate
connotations when used to refer to government departments or
areas where official power is exercised. If we are to use it, then it is
better to use the term either without qualification as referring to the
Gospel witness and mission of the whole church rather than limited
to particular groups or roles. Speaking of the ordained person as 'the
minister' is thus confusing or at best unfortunate, because it can be
taken to mean that Gospel witness and work belongs to no one else or
that the laity's calling is simply to help the minister or be ministered
to. Thus it is helpful to emphasize that ministry or *diakonia* is that
which is shared by all baptized members of the Church and exercised
by lay and ordained alike but in different ways. Ministry belongs to
the whole church. All are called to *love and serve the Lord* and to *bear
witness.*

The lay life and the different ordained roles are thus forms of
diakonia. They are also expressions of the servanthood of Jesus Christ

and of the Church which include what have been traditionally known as the *Three Offices of Christ (Figure 4.4)*:

- Prophet – witness to the truth of the Gospel and the exploration of faith.
- Priest – worship and praise to the God who has saved us and the offering of new life to all.
- King – making present the saving power and authority of God in all human affairs.

Underlying all three offices is the role of Christ as Servant. This is the option for the poor and needy: service to all. Power and authority exercised for the sake of the Kingdom and the common good not for personal gain. This is an especially important part of *King* so that Christ and all appointed people exercise this role as service and as servants.

The idea of the *Three Offices of Christ* theology is a very ancient way of representing the Church which goes back to the early church[2] and is, of course, based upon the titles of Jesus that the New Testament writers record for us and which have been fruitfully explored by many biblical commentators including R. H. Fuller, Oscar Cullmann and J. G. Dunn. The *Three Offices* theology inspired such writers as Yves Congar in his major works on the role of the laity in the Church,[3] which has had enormous impact ecumenically in thinking about the priesthood of all the baptized, as well as being a fundamental theme in Roman Catholic theology in the documents of Vatican II[4] and the Methodist statement on the Church *Called to Love and Praise*.[5] This theology has also been key in ecumenical studies of the liturgy. However, it is also found in the Anglican Divines of the seventeenth century, notably Pearson's *Exposition of the Creed* where he suggests that all Christians have some participation in the offices of Christ through being members of *His Body*. In other words, we need to link Christology with ecclesiology when thinking about the nature of the

---

[2] For example, Tertullian, Hippolytus, Cyril, Gregory Nazianzan, Eusebius, Augustine of Hippo.

[3] *Lay People in the Church*, London 1959 and *Priest and Layman*, London: DLT, 1967.

[4] All the faithful by baptism 'are in their own way made sharers in the priestly, prophetic and kingly functions of Christ' in Decree *Lumen Gentium* para 31 in Abbott (ed.) *The Documents of Vatican II*, London 1967 cf also 'the laity, too, share in the priestly, prophetic, and royal office of Christ and therefore have their own role to play in the mission of the whole People of God in the Church and in the world' (*Apostolicam Actuositatem*) para 2.

[5] Adopted by the Methodist Conference in 1999.

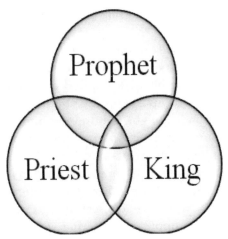

Figure 4:4 The Three Offices of Christ

Church and the various roles within it. What is offered, then, is a kind of three-legged stool (more stable than a four legged-one!). The legs must each be kept in balance or the whole structure collapses.

The theme of all these writers is this: although the figures of the Old Testament foreshadow the Messiah or Anointed One, when Christ comes, he surpasses all of them. He fulfils all expectations, not simply as the best example of each role but as the paradigm of Prophet, Priest and King. Each individual Christian as participating in the Body of Christ, shares also in these *Three Offices* as does the Church as a whole but as *King* Jesus is also *Servant* (Mk 10.45), as *Priest* he offers, but is also that which is offered (Heb. 9.11), as *Prophet,* he teaches but is also a model of obedience to his Father, listening to Him (Mk 6.14-15 and John 14.24). In other words, Jesus becomes for us the model of how power and role should be exercised in the Church.

All participate in these *offices* but in different ways and with different emphases. The lay (i.e. non-ordained role) is particularly prophetic in that we are all charged to challenge and witness to Christ wherever we are. The layperson is sent out from the Church to do this.

One of the most important exponents of this theology was John Henry Newman in a sermon which he published in *Sermons on Subjects of the Day.* For him the prophet combines 'deep reflection and inventive genius' so as to 'extend the range of our knowledge' and 'introduce us into new worlds', the priest suffers, denies himself and offers his life in service and sacrifice for others, the king puts ideas into practice, makes things happen, realizes what must be done, and leads the people forward while modelling ethical conduct and servanthood.

However, he also notices some paradoxes: if Christ triumphs, he does so through suffering, humiliation and service; if he was a teacher, he was also humble and despised; if he was wise and royal, he also led a life of hardship like the shepherds; if he was a person of wisdom, reflection and thought withdrawing into the wilderness, he also acted in the world, involving himself with humankind.

Christ, then, is our pattern of what he calls 'contrary modes of life'. Newman suggests that the ministerial orders in a special way exemplify this pattern of Christ, although their members are earthen vessels. As Apostles, they are consecrated to suffer and endure with the poor and the oppressed, offering worship to God but also teaching under the guidance of the Holy Spirit, ruling and governing with love, not like conquerors of the earth: 'weak without armies, without strongholds, naked, defenceless', yet rulers because as they are also preachers and teachers, appealing to reason and the heart, eliciting rather than coercing obedience to the Gospel. They are like soldiers but shedding no blood but their own; teachers who are also disciples, acting out their own precepts; rulers but without pomp. The role of the Church and all its members is 'to speak, to do and to suffer' and this is the calling of all the baptized who can be called 'shadows of Christ':

> All of us are bound, according to our opportunities – first to learn the truth; and moreover, we must not only know, but we must impart our knowledge. Nor only so, but next we must bear witness to the truth ... This was the new thing that Christ brought into the world, a heavenly doctrine, a system of holy and supernatural truths, which are to be received and transmitted for he is our Prophet, maintained even unto suffering after his pattern, who is our Priest, and obeyed, for he is our King.[6]

Newman and others who have made use of this metaphor have emphasized the important of balance: each of these *offices* need each other otherwise the Church and its ministry become distorted. Order as represented by the office of *King* can easily become tyranny, that of the *Prophet*' reason without real faith, *Priest* can become superstition or bigotry. The task of leadership here is to balance ministry with due emphasis on all three, allowing each to influence the others.

How, therefore, should ministry be described? It is the service and witness of the Gospel that we do on behalf of Christ for others.

---

[6] *Sermons Bearing on Subjects of the Day* V, Rivingtons, London 1868 p. 62.

This may be done alone, with others or under the direction of other people. It belongs, as we have seen, to the whole church and ultimately Christ for we are his hands and his feet. All true ministry is thus done in his name and presided over by Him. It does not belong to a given group but is very much gift related and is also an expression of the fact that each of us has a vocation, a mission to which we are called as members of the Christian community. It is therefore misleading to describe the ordained person as *the minister* or the ordained role as *the ministry* for the ordained person may, in fact, be a receiver of ministry. Restricting the meaning in this way is an impoverishment of the term. It is also misleading to see the difference between ordained and lay ministry as that of leadership and those who are led, since lay leadership is an important part of Gospel witness and work.

Contemporary studies of the New Testament teaching on ministry and leadership note that there ministry is normally done with other people rather than alone.[7] Indeed the *lone ranger* model of leadership that seems to have become more and more the norm over time is abnormal in the very early history of the Church. An important meaning of the term *collaborative ministry* must therefore mean the different ways in which the People of God work together to bring Christ to the world and to each other. It should not be restricted to clergy teams or even appointed teams of clergy and laity, although these will be important forms of it.

One of the tasks of a church is to help people to realize their giftedness as baptized ministers called by God and to use them in the service of others *with others* so as to maximize their strengths and counterbalance any weaknesses. This will be explored further when considering team working. Modelling collaborative styles of working is now increasingly seen not just as a better way of doing things, but as integral to the notion of church and a sign of the Gospel because it emphasizes the importance of an ecclesiology based on relatedness rather than hierarchy. A church community with a strong sense of this will itself be a sign of the Gospel and a collective witness to it. The roles of deacon, presbyter and bishop are thus forms or orders of the priesthood that all share. That is not to diminish their importance or distinctiveness but to stress their common nature with all Christian people and the endeavour that all must share.

---

[7] E.g. Tiller, ibid. p. 57.

LEADERSHIP

One of the distinctive features of the Church is that there are two kinds of leadership.

These will be referred to as:

Functional and gift-related, in which a person seeks to accomplish a task through coordinating the work of others. There are many different forms of this. Executive functions belong here.

Ecclesially symbolic in which something is being said about the nature of what it means to be church through the role, i.e. it makes an ecclesial statement, independently of the style or character of the individual fulfilling it. This is what is meant by the term *office* in connection with ordination.

Both lay and ordained members will exercise the first but the latter is peculiar to the ordained roles. While holders of these roles will also fulfil functional and gift related leadership, it does not follow that all those who perform functional leadership within the church are making an ecclesial statement in the same way. It is also important not to see the roles of, for example, deacon, presbyter and bishop primarily as the chief executives of the Church although for various reasons they will have to do some executive functions, for that is to undervalue their ecclesially symbolic roles. Archdeacons in the Anglican Church perhaps do more of this.

FUNCTIONAL AND GIFT-RELATED LEADERSHIP

This is directly related to the gifts, which an individual person has. The ordained person will be gifted at some forms of functional leadership but not others. It should thus not be too readily assumed that the ordained person(s) must necessarily perform certain historical functional leadership roles, e.g. chairing meetings, which is a functional role.

However, which functional leadership roles those who hold ecclesially symbolic positions will perform, will be determined by the strengths and weaknesses of the community as a whole and the context in which ministry is to be exercised as well as by his/her own capabilities.

Though linked to management, leadership in this sense is different from it. This kind of functional leadership may be done collaboratively as in a team as well as in more traditional ways. A useful distinction between leadership and management, as we have seen, is that leadership is about doing the *right thing*, management is about *doing them right* or, put another way, leadership is about what we do and management about doing them properly. The two are linked, but it will be seen that leadership is about seeing the big picture and being strategic, management is more about seeing the detail and ensuring effective follow through.

Although the ordained leadership of a church will need to be involved in both of these appropriately, these do not by any means encompass the ordained role. The heresy of the *lone ranger* model is that it absorbs both the functional and the ecclesially symbolic roles, treating them as one.

Key functional leadership tasks are:

- coordinating parts to the whole
- team building
- communication of vision in a way that makes it realizable
- motivating
- valuing and affirming team members
- balancing the needs of tasks, groups and individuals
- strategic planning
- consultation and effective decision-making processes
- oversight of progress.

Key management tasks are:

- administration
- implementation
- making resources available
- responding to need
- record keeping
- monitoring progress
- quality control
- maintaining channels of communication
- staff relations.

Important though all these are, none of these are specifically integral to the ordained role and can be appropriately done by both lay and ordained members of the Church. In essence, they are no different from any other organization. It can be argued however, that the ordained persons have a particular responsibility to ensure that these functional and gift related leadership roles, which are related to the ministry of all, are done in accordance with Gospel values.

It has been suggested earlier that the term *ecclesially symbolic* is used to indicate that this kind of leadership says something about the nature of the Church and are, in some way a permanent sign of that. To it we can add the term *presidential* but it is a word used very differently here from the US where the President is an all-powerful executive. In this context it is used in the sense of *sitting before or in front of.*

It is a signful or sacramental role in the sense that the role makes present what it signifies for the Church. It is independent of the character of the person who fulfils this office and is not so much a position of power as of influence. Nevertheless, it is an important form of leadership a bit like spiritual leadership. However, it is part of the role to see that executive functions are done.

The keyword here is servant and the metaphor of Christ washing his disciples' feet, which suggests that this type of leadership is one of humility and service to those who are already ministering, a role of making ministry possible, of animating it and supporting it (cf. Mk 10.45).

It is a role of being rather than doing. Some action, e.g. in the liturgy are *presidential* because they are particularly *ecclesially significant* and it is therefore appropriate that the office holder should perform them. Moreover, it is a dedicated role in which a person in some sense is set apart for this purpose. It is a role of *being for* the ecclesial community in an important sense. This can be exercised collegially and usually was in the early church.

The following are key presidential roles:

- Icon – bearer of meaning and coherence, custodian of community symbols and wisdom.
- Interpreter – of the vision and the tradition for the community, holding the community narrative. The weaver of new patterns.
- Focus – for unity and co-inherence.
- Representative – local to the wider church, wider church to the local church, making the one present to the other, i.e. a sign of catholicity.
- Exemplar – of Gospel vision of values, and of style. *Holds up* the Gospel to the people, which confronts them but also challenges them to be prophetic.
- Overview – *Episcope* – holds the ring, seeing the interrelationship of the Church and communicating this to all its parts.

- Setter of climate – the feel of what it means to be church and how we are a community. In touch with the roots of the Christian communion, its life, its worship and mission.
- Servant – of the Church's mission, worship and ministry, enabling and facilitating them to happen.
- Apostolic presence – expresses solidarity with Apostolic past and living witness with others in the presidential role.

It follows, that if the presidential role is not primarily a functional one (but will have some functions attached to it), and ministry is the responsibility of the whole church rather than its ordained persons, then the ordained should see their position not as *doers* of the Church's ministry but as animators of it or 'servants of its ministers'. Suenens, applying this to the Roman Catholic Church, argued that:

> Bishops, priests and deacons are not defined first and foremost by their exercise of sacramental cult but rather in terms of their various responsibilities in regard to the evangelisation of the world.[8]

Although the non-conformist traditions have different ecclesiologies to those with an episcopal structure, the presidential role, as defined above, is still there but may be exercised collectively, e.g. the Methodist Conference with its annually elected President as well as through its local and national connexional structures. There are different ways of exercising *episcope*.

APPLICATIONS

Three examples of ecclesially significant roles, which illustrate the model in the episcopal-led churches will now be discussed. However, the model is adaptable to other situations and ecclesiologies where values and vision need to be held in trust and communicated. Indeed, this is true even of secular organizations. Charles Handy, for example, in his study of organizations talks of the importance of the *ambassadorial* or *representative* character of leadership and that this is a key factor in the effectiveness of the position.[9] Handy also stresses the importance of leaders modelling values. He writes:

> We cannot avoid the role of model once we have any importance in the world. Since modelling is thrust upon us it would be well for us to consider what forms

---

[8] Ibid. p. 157.
[9] Handy, Charles (1985) *Understanding Organizations* (3rd edn) London: Penguin pp. 111ff.

of behaviour, what attitudes and values, we represent. If we are seen as effective then these behaviours and values will be imitated, if ineffective they will be shunned. Either way we influence behaviour.[10]

If the representative and modelling aspect of leadership is important in almost any kind of organization, it becomes more and more important in ones which seek to promote, communicate and uphold values such as charities and faith communities. This is done in two main ways: by the way in which the someone exercises their leadership role and by the nature of the office itself. These are clearly closely connected although distinct but if a person behaves in such a way as to negate the very meaning of the office they hold then the damage done to the credibility of the vision itself, is immense. Conversely, the sign that is given by a great leader is significantly enhanced by the manner in which the office is exercised.

Following the Lima texts, we can apply this to the three roles of bishop, deacon and priest as follows.

THE BISHOP

Bishops preach the Word, preside at the sacraments and administer discipline in such a way as to be representative pastoral ministers of oversight, contiguity and unity in the Church. They have pastoral oversight of the area to which they are called. They serve the apostolicity and unity of the Church's teaching, worship and sacramental life. They have responsibility for leadership in the Church's mission. They relate the Christian community in their area to the wider church, and the universal church to their community.[11]

This is particularly an apostolic role and a representative one in which the one, holy, Catholic and apostolic church is made present in a region through the office.

The bishop, particularly the *bearer* of the Church like a founder member and, rather like trustees, are custodians of the meaning of *church.*

As *icon*, the office is a bearer of meaning and the role is to manifest that. The position is one of interpreting Gospel tradition with fellow bishops but also as in touch with the instinct for truth which is possessed by the *Laos*, the whole church. The importance of being a focus for unity of local churches one with another and their communion with worldwide church, is integral to the role also,

[10] Ibid. p. 113.

[11] 'Ministry', Section III C. para 28 in *Baptism, Eucharist and Ministry*, Faith and Order Paper No. 111, World Council of Churches, Geneva (1982).

so that the office holder is representative of the whole church and of the local to the wider church. This is done through oversight of the community and of whole church, animating ministry, giving it expression and direction, rooting it in apostolic tradition by being in communion with his fellow bishops as well as *in communion* with his fellow leaders and the whole People of God.

The bishop should be the symbol, *par excellence* of the principle that the true leader 'will find his place when he has succeeded in helping the others find theirs' since his seat in his cathedral is rarely occupied, a symbol in itself, unlike the presbyter who frequently occupies his stall. The bishop, in a real sense, has *no place* to fulfil much of his role, being more like the shepherd going from place to place with his flock. He returns to *his place* when emphasizing the iconic, apostolic foundational office that he has, particularly when he has been helping his ministers (the whole *laos*) find their ministry. Not 'putting them in their place' but finding *a place* where they are, or accompanying them on their journey to find it. The bishop does not *take the place* of others when he visits a church but comes as a pilgrim to find his place along with others as servant as well as shepherd.

As was noted in the last chapter, one of the best reflections on this aspect of the role of bishop comes from the pen of Pope Gregory I in his *Regula Pastoralis*.[12] Gregory begins the work by giving a general warning to anyone who covets such a position as that of a bishop, tempting though it is, now that Christianity is becoming respectable. Already Gregory has noticed that there are people who like the position. Simony, after all, became quite a problem in the medieval church. It is a highly skilled office and Gregory himself laments his own unskillfulnes. An unskilled pastor is like an incompetent doctor. However, Gregory warns against people who have all the learning but none of the practice of spiritual precepts. Such a person is like someone who fouls with their feet the water that the sheep will drink, quoting Ezekiel 34.18-19 in the second chapter.

The example of Christ should warn us and give us an example of the heavy burden of government and the need to approach it with a spirit of self-sacrifice. He refused to be made a king and so

---

[12] 'Regula Pastoralis', *A Select Library of Nicene and Post-Nicene Fathers of the Christian Church*, second series, Vols XII and XIII, Oxford and New York, (1895). The text follows that of Migne in Patrologia, Vol LXXVII and was translated by Rev. James Barmby with an introduction, notes and indices. All references are to this edition.

a bishop should avoid any temptation to delight in supreme rule. Perhaps with himself in mind, Gregory warns us about the problems of government: it is difficult to be occupied with the many different things which government demands. These dissipate the mind which then neglects self-knowledge and understanding. It is rather like going on a journey, he says, and then becoming so preoccupied that you forget where you are going and so becoming estranged from self-examination, becoming blind to what is happening. Gregory cites several OT figures like Hezekiah as good examples of this. Some people, though, says Gregory could profit others by their example of supreme rule but prefer the easy life and so the Church loses a good pastor. It is right to avoid high office through humility but not to avoid it if it is the will of God (chapters 4–6).

Those who covet high office, Gregory notes shrewdly, often mentally propose to themselves all sorts of good works but actually never do them (Chapter 9). So what sort of person ought to be made a bishop? He needs to be a person who already lives a spiritual life, who has died to all the passions of the flesh, disregards worldly prosperity, who fears no adversity, who does not covet anything of other people's but gives freely of what he possesses, who is compassionate and quickly moved to forgive, yet also a firm upholder of rectitude, who lives the virtuous life but also abhors vice as if committed by himself, who sympathizes with the infirmities of others but also rejoices in their goodness and strives to live and teach by example.

But the pastor is also someone who waters dry hearts with the streams of right doctrine. He is a man of prayer and contemplation and must know God so as to be able to intercede for the people. In a kind of allegorical interpretation of the illnesses common in his time, Gregory uses images of ailments like blindness, deformities of various kinds, and even impetigo as ways of thinking about the moral obstacles to the kind of example that the good pastor must give and the skills he must be able to deploy. The pastor must be someone of spiritual health as well as highly skilled.

Gregory's second part explores how the chief pastor should live. Good example in all spiritual things is to be expected but his emphasis on approachability and the need for compassion is very marked. Using the example of Jacob's ladder (Gen. 27.12) upon which angels ascend and descend, the true preacher must ascend constantly towards God but descend always moved by the Spirit of God to those who are in trouble who will naturally want to turn to him (Chapter 6). The pastor is also warned not to be so preoccupied with the external works of governance that he neglects the spiritual nor so preoccupied with the spiritual that he neglects his duties to those who have been entrusted to him. Gregory has two kinds of people in mind: those who exult in secular concerns who 'count it a pleasure to be tired by action' and who 'delight in being hustled by worldly tumults'[13] for such leaders are unable to help their people spiritually but neither are the second group of people who 'undertake the care of the flock but desire to be so at leisure for their own spiritual concerns'[14] that they equally neglect the needs of those who are put under them. It is all about balance.

It should be no surprise that Gregory ends this reflection with an emphasis on the importance of study, particularly of Scripture, for the pastor is a teacher and a preacher, ever ready to help his flock to understand and live the Gospel. In a lovely image, Gregory likens the Church to the Ark of the Covenant which was carried by staves fitted into four gold rings at the corners, so that it could be equipped for journey to the four quarters of the world. The staves must always be in the rings, he suggests, as a sign of the readiness to preach and to teach, which comes about by continual meditation on the words of Scripture. 'Strong and persevering teachers, as incorruptible pieces of timber, are to be sought for, who by cleaving ever to instruction out of the sacred volumes [of the Gospels] may declare the unity of the holy Church', he says. Gregory is clear that it is by teaching and preaching that the Gospel is brought to unbelievers and this means that 'those who attend upon the office of preaching should not recede from the study of sacred lore'.[15] The spiritual health of the pastor is thus vital for the spiritual well-being of those for whom he has responsibility. What is a critical question for the right fulfilment of the office that he holds. It is an iconic role which succeeds often despite the woundedness of the office holder, and as such glimpses a direction and a different way of looking at the world and at the self.[16]

THE DEACON

The model here is that of permanent deacon rather than the preparatory role for ordination to the presbyterate and, as such, is being

---

[13] Ibid. Part II Chapter VII.

[14] Ibid.

[15] Ibid. Part II Chapter XI.

[16] Cf the important discussion by Rowan Williams (2000) *Lost Icons*, T & T Clark, pp. 184 ff. The wounded pastor is of course famously explored by Graham Greene in *The Power and the Glory.*

rediscovered by the churches in recent decades. According to the Lima text in *Baptism, Eucharist and Ministry:*

> Deacons represent to the Church its calling as servant in the world. By struggling with the myriad needs of societies and persons they exemplify the interdependence of worship and service in the Church's life.[17]

He or she works with the members of the Church in caring for the poor, the needy, the sick and all who are in trouble, i.e. exemplifies the Church's option for the poor and the marginalized.

The deacon is a participant especially in the role and ministry of the bishop and therefore shares in an important way in his/her presidency as servant and builder of all servant ministry within a region. This is more clearly seen in a permanent diaconate as is now found in the Non-conformist and Roman Catholic churches today rather than in the diaconate which is a stepping stone to the presbyterate. He or she is a sign to the Church of its servant calling and to those in governance never to forget this or allow power to be misused. The deacon upholds the Gospel (enacted liturgically in some traditions when a deacon reads the Gospel and preaches). The diaconal role will often be found in various forms of selfless, practical service, in the 'option for the poor' within the secular community. It is a reminder to the whole church that it is in the world but not of it and must get its hands dirty if God's love is to be brought to all humankind, especially the poor and the needy.

Of course, in an important sense, *all* ministry is diaconal whether clerical or lay but if it is true to say that humans cannot live by bread alone, they still need bread. The Gospel is to be upheld by humble service not just by oral proclamation. It is this that the deacon exemplifies especially.

THE PRESBYTER

> Presbyters serve as pastoral ministers of Word and sacraments in a local eucharistic community. They are preachers and teachers of the faith, exercise pastoral care, and bear responsibility for the discipline of the congregation to the end that the world may believe that the entire membership of the Church may be renewed, strengthened and equipped in ministry.[18]

This might be described as *collegial presidency of a local community* in common with fellow ordained persons but collaborating also with

---

[17] Faith and Order Paper No 111 para 31.
[18] Ibid. para 30.

the whole People of God. Its particular focus is that of Word and Sacrament but is also one of energizing and animating a Christian community and leading it forward. It is a *presidency of tension* because:

> a priest must always live out a twofold demand: to be in the world and not of it, to understand it and oppose it, to love it and to contradict it.[19]

They have a particular focus in preaching, teaching, pastoral care, good governance and equipping the People of God for ministry, presiding over these as functions in which many people may be involved *in a locale.*

Particular functions will accrue to the presbyter because of what he or she is but these will essentially be very few. Most can be done by others but the symbolic roles cannot. The presbyter shares all these roles with the bishop as part of a wider *episcope* and may share this in another sense if the presbyter has oversight of more than one church as is increasingly the case in many parts of Europe.

If one of the most important roles of the presbyter is to animate and to be the servant of the ministry of the whole People of God in a locale then the tambourine model is much more relevant than the pyramid. The continuity of a parish, church or chapel is constituted by the people who are its members in communion with their presidential leadership who is in turn in collegial communion with the bishop and him with the wider church. While the presbyteral role is essential, an ecclesial locale will never be without ministry as long as the people have a sense of their calling and are allowed to exercise it appropriately. The problem of the do-it-all minister is that ministry is in danger of collapse in times of crisis or when reorganizations become inevitable. It also denies the laity their proper role in or for the Church.

IMPLICATIONS

This model attempts to offer an alternative to the functional one which sees the ordained person as the *doers* of ministry and puts in its place a more ontological one, in which the ordained person becomes the servant and animator of ministry in all its various forms. It seeks also to do justice to the priesthood of all believers by beginning with what we all have in common, which is discipleship and ministerial gifting, which it is the role of the ordained to resource. The fact that

---

[19] Ibid. p. 109.

ministry belongs to us all helps in growing a mature, adult church which shares leadership and ministry.

It enables us to see the ordained as open also to being led and ministered to as well as someone who will have ministerial and leadership gifts themselves. The role of the ordained undergirds the community and its work for the Gospel rather than rising above it in a position of power. Yet it is also authoritative in rooting the local church in its apostolic past and in its communion with the wider church. It does this by seeing these roles first in terms of symbols and metaphor and only then in other leadership terms. It distinguishes between what may have to be done because of the role from what has to be done by someone because of need. There are very few things that an ordained person has to do because of the role and these are usually confined to things, which it is appropriate to do because of the significance of the role and its signful character.

Seeing ministry in this way counters the autocratic *lone ranger* model of ministry, which regards it as primarily the role of the ordained acting alone, replacing it by one which stresses collegiality and the need to realize the gifts of all, honouring the distinctive vocation of each Christian which is nurtured and promoted in partnership with other members of the church and with the worldwide church also.

QUESTIONS

- What do you see as the implications both locally and in the Church as a whole for an emphasis on ministry as the responsibility of the whole People of God?
- Would this require a change of culture?
- How helpful is the distinction between functional leadership and ecclesiologically symbolic leadership.
- Are there problems in trying to bring theological language and management language together?
- What issues are there for collaborative ways of working in the Church?
- How helpful is it to use the *Three Offices of Christ* image for thinking about balance of role and function in the Church?

Chapter 5

LEADERSHIP IN CHANGE

To live is to change, to be perfect is to have changed often. (J. H. Newman)
Life is a series of lesser deaths which men call change. (H. Belloc)

These two quotations help us to recognize that change should be considered normal and also in many ways to be welcomed. Perfection is achieved through successfully negotiating change to reach a position of fulfilment, of becoming what we are and can be. We are human but we have to spend our lives also *becoming* human to reach what some theologians have called the *humanum*. Being human is thus always *work in progress*. The quotation from Belloc reminds us that for this to happen there must be a letting go of the past situation if a new one is to emerge. Death precedes life here as autumn and winter precede spring and summer. We have continually to be *born again* in order to move forward and this can often be painful and difficult not just for individuals but also for groups, institutions and nations.

Leadership in change is the real test of any leader. Successful navigation of the hazards of bringing in a new order of things or responding to circumstances that demand different ways of doing and being require skill, discernment and wisdom in a way that simple maintenance of the status quo does not, for so many variables have to be kept in focus. This is all the more true of the Church which has also the task of remaining true to its founding vision, core values and historic roots and of responding to the here and now and a beckoning future. Change may be being urged upon it, which is unfaithful to the Gospel or, on the other hand, the Church may fall into infidelity by failing to change when it is clear that to do so would be what the Gospel requires. Thus the leadership of the Church is always faced with the question: Is this change an authentic expression of the Gospel? This is quite different from asking whether this or that innovation will work or judging change by some kind of economic or utilitarian outcome. Often the answer is not clear and so the Church may have to go forward in trust but having the courage to put things right, if the innovation should prove to be a mistake in terms of the Gospel.

The world is going through very rapid change, the like of which has never been seen before. How the Church responds to this is a crucial question and the answers will depend on how it sees itself at any time in terms of being *in the world but not of it*. In what circumstances should it stand as a beacon of continuity or even opposition in the face of change and how far should it allow itself to be changed by forces outside it? God's grace and work is not confined to the Church but needs to be recognized wherever it may be, but it is equally true that the Church is always in need of renewal and the impetus for this may come from outside as well as from within; hence the need for discernment and listening to other voices than our own. Discernment is also needed to distinguish between change that is also development and takes a group constructively onwards and change which is really more of the same or a form of negative growth.

The American writer, Gilbert Rendle, in his book *Leading Change in the Congregation* suggests two ways that change can be described: *linear* and *chaos*.[1] Linear change occurs when something is wrong, needs attention and a replacement or rebuild can solve the problem. Looking at the *as is* of a situation and the anticipated vision of the future can suggest aims and an action plan. Rendle describes this as a linear-type process of growth through change. Five-year plans or fixing a faulty component on a photocopier are examples of linear changes. However, there is another agenda of change, which these types of activities cannot effect. Rendle calls this *chaos change* and it occurs when life changes take place, such as marriage or bereavement, or a paradigm shift begins to arise. This type of change requires a different response, one which might be epitomized in the phrase 'looking at the world through different eyes'. What is needed is a change of perspective and attitude, getting used to living in a different way. Linear changes may form part of the new way, but they cannot replace what is requisite to chaos change. It is necessary to see things differently.

---

[1] Rendle, Gilbert R. (1998) *Leading Change in the Congregation*. Washington, DC: The Alban Institute Publishing, pp. 77–103.

The Anglican report, *Mission Shaped Church,* began to hint at this when it suggested *fresh expressions* of church, but the hearts and minds of people in church will likely take more than a report's findings to persuade them of the need for change. The ecclesiology-in-practice in churches, parishes, circuits, districts and dioceses is not one which can be changed quickly. Chaos is an apt term for the confusion that is apparent in many churches as they grapple with the challenges of the twenty-first century, but chaos can also be regarded as an equally accurate technical term, signifying a higher agenda of bereavement and change, which requires a certain style of process to resolve.

Rendle uses the metaphor of wilderness to define chaos change, signifying the biblical journey from Egypt to the Promised Land. It is quite possible that the nature of the change, which is still occurring in the Church, is perceived as linear while in fact it is chaotic. Looking at the problem through a linear lens means attempting to fix the ministerial training provision, adding in lay training to resource the clerical recruitment pool, ordaining many new priests without adequate training, reversing the decline in leadership and membership numbers through emphasis on mission; measuring the educational provision with academic measurements (degrees, etc.). All the signs appear to point towards an approach based on an assumption of linear change. However, considering the muddle of ecclesiology, the confusion about theologies of ordination, laity and ministry, the lack of definition of mission, and the skewed projections of statistics, chaos change appears to describe the situation precisely. What is needed is strategic and prophetic thinking, in essence a re-membering of the role and theology of the laity in church is vital to its future.

In all this, leaders need to think strategically and to be able to discern what may be required, striking a balance between:

- *steady state* (maintenance) or keeping things as they are so that all that is required is to trim the ship
- *innovation or development* which may require a radical reorientation of the Church or group
- *chaos management* which may mean venturing into the unknown, adopting radical ways forward with a strong element of risk
- *policy-making* and ensuring that clear aims and goals are formulated and communicated.

When innovation or crisis management is required, accurate diagnosis is important so the questions 'What kind of change may be needed here?' and 'What is at stake?' become key. Two options must be considered:

Option 1

Regulate and rectify: seeing congregations as a structure with parts and a whole that may need to be fine tuned:

- putting it right or repair
- repair/adapt and learning something new
- learning to be different and to do things differently.

Option 2

Look, understand and respond: seeing congregations as evolving organisms which will require the ability:

- to think laterally
- to respond to the challenge of *wild or chaos change*
- to cope with uncertainty and gradually emerging insight.

The options above require different kinds of leadership. The first requires the skills of structured planning, the second the skills of eliciting trust and hope in the search for the way forward. The latter, especially, will require lateral thinking but also a sense of a covenantal relationship and faithful living with considerable attention to resourcing relationships. Both kinds of leadership will require attention to feelings, unconscious processes, norms, cultural factors, risk taking and human climate change. But many people would argue today that leadership for the wilderness experience is what is required above all for the Church in the twenty-first century although the two types of change are not mutually exclusive; successful leadership of chaos change will allow linear planning to take place but with an element of provisionality about it.

PREPARING FOR CHANGE

The parables of the seeds and the sower in Matthew 13 provide a very helpful metaphor for understanding some aspects of leadership in change. In these images, Jesus is exploring why the word of the kingdom sometimes takes root and at other times does not. To a people used to the hardships of growing food, five variables would have come to mind to help them understand the point that Jesus was making. These are: climate, the seasons, the soil, the seed and the skill of the sower. Applied to change, this sees the task of leadership as one of cultivation (Figure 5:1).

Climate: Predominant weather patterns, temperature. What will grow here and what will not: knowing the context and the environment.

Seasons: A time to sow and a time to reap. Are the conditions right?

Soil: Knowing the ground and doing effective soil preparation. Feeding the soil.

Seed: The quality and nature of what is to be sown. Will it grow and will it grow here?

Sower: The skills of knowing when, what and how to sow; this is a form of practical wisdom: doing the *right thing*, at the *right time* and in the *right way*, in the *right context* and nurturing it to fruition.

Like seed sowing, leadership in change is a real skill or rather a set of skills and reflection on experience. Church leaders must know and understand the predominant weather patterns of the people among whom they work. They may need to begin to change these before particular forms of change become possible. What are the norms here? What are the warm, growth enhancing parts of the community, and which seem to be cold and unpromising? What are the predominant values and how are they expressed? Are they changing and why? These are among the kind of questions that need to be asked, particularly prior to any initiative of linear change.

Discerning when the conditions are right for a change then becomes a crucial issue. Many a worthwhile initiative has founded because of bad timing. Above all, ground preparation or helping the people to be ready for change by enabling them to let go of the familiar and to develop

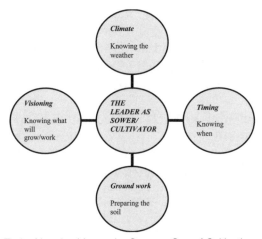

Figure 5:1 The Task of Leadership can be Seen as One of Cultivation

the courage for the new. It may mean breaking the change down into bite-sized chunks or having prior experience of smaller change which is successfully managed and seen to be beneficial and confidence building, will be helpful here as preparation for something more challenging.

Attitudes and values may need to be worked on as well as opportunities for participation in consultation, decision-making and exchanging information and understanding the likely benefits. So much experience of change or reorganization in today's world is perceived negatively, as change for change's sake, or because the last change was a disaster and painful or without discernible benefit. This leads to resistance to change.

Focusing on the norms and the underlying culture of an organization can be very helpful here. Broadly speaking, there are two kinds of organizational culture: *open or closed*.[2] These terms were originally employed by a family therapist, Virginia Satir in a book called *People-making*. In her book she described families in terms of systems by which she meant that they consist of several individual parts that are essential and related to each other in order to achieve certain desirable outcomes that are the result of actions and reactions. An organization, especially a church, is rather like this. The characteristics of an *open or closed*, system can be adapted from her thinking as follows:

OPEN

- *Basic assumption*: most people are basically good and consequently should be given trust and respect as persons and their membership valued.
- The self-worth of each is a very important emphasis in all dealings between leaders and the led and between colleagues.
- The exercise of power and authority in the organization always seeks to value people and their gifts and skills, not negate them.
- Actions and decisions are based on objective reality and informed data.
- Communication at all levels of the Church is open, direct and honest, i.e. assertive.
- Rules and regulations are relevant, appropriate and open to review as circumstances and needs alter. There will be established ways of doing this known to all.

---

[2] Satir, V. (1972) *People-making*. California: Science and Behavior Books Inc, pp. 112ff.

- Change is considered normal and viewed positively. This is most likely to be developmental change that builds on the past.

Closed

- *Basic assumption*: most people are basically weak or bad and have continually to be regulated and controlled to function correctly.
- Relationships between people usually have to be backed up by force or the fear of it, so an emphasis on jurisdiction and compliance will be paramount.
- Might is right so that the exercise for power is usually arbitrary and not open to question. The leadership cannot be questioned or challenged.
- People are not trusted to know what may be best for them, thus fostering a dependency culture, especially on the clergy.
- Communication is usually indirect and predominantly of a blaming or placatory nature, i.e. submissive or aggressive.
- Rules are inflexible and often out of date. Tradition is seen as precedent.
- Change is usually resisted as unnecessary, so that attempts to make suggestions for it are subverted or simply disallowed.

Few organizations or communities are wholly one or other of these but there may be sufficient of the *closed* organization features in the whole or some of its parts to make change extremely difficult. Therefore, something has to be done to change the underlying culture and norms before linear change can be undertaken. It is on this that the cultivator/leader must focus for whether a church is an *open* or *closed* organization will directly impact on morale which needs to be constantly kept in view by the leadership.

Looking at a church in this way can be an uncomfortable experience as there is always a gap between what we profess to believe, our practice and the reality. The leader and the congregation may be aware of the gap and be trying to do something about it, but they may also be unaware of discrepancies, some of which may be quite basic. Put in other terms, borrowed from reflective practice, there is always some gap between our accepted theology (what we profess) and our theology-in-practice (how we act in fact). The familiar Johari Window (Figure 5:2) is one way of illustrating this because it takes into account not only what the members of an organization cannot see but also what those outside it cannot perceive either but which may still affect behaviour:

Open to me and to others	Known to me but hidden from others
(The visible congregation or church.)	(The congregation or church we see but which is not visible to others.)
Blind to me but not to others	Unknown to me or others/unconscious
(The congregation or church that *outsiders* see but the members do not.)	(The hidden reality of which all are unaware.)

Figure 5:2 The Johari Window

These *rooms* can of course be of different *sizes*. A church congregation may have very little that is actually visible or open to view and have a great deal of which it is unaware but that is seen by others. On the other hand, a very open church or congregation may try to make as much of its life as transparent and visible as possible.

The more an organization seeks insight into itself and to close the gap between how it sees itself and how others see it, the greater will be its capacity to deal with change in a positive manner and to narrow the divide between the theology that is professed and the theology that is acted or carried out. This requires structured reflection.

LINEAR CHANGE

By and large, linear change is well structured and more in the control of those who lead it. The process can be set out as a cyclical process which is ongoing (Figure 5:3).

The first stage must be an exercise in exploration and reflection to consider these issues in which there are eight stages.

UNDERSTANDING OURSELVES IN OUR CONTEXT

Here a church community will look at its immediate as well as the wider context in order to understand how it relates to the locale and what issues and factors it should be considering.

This may involve some sociological analysis because no church that seeks to be *in* the world but not of it can think about the future without asking *in what world is it?* A model of how to do this was put forward in the Church of England Report *Faith in the City* which it called *An Audit for the Local Church.*[3] While this audit, as it is set out, may be more than most church congregations have the resources

---

[3] *Faith in the City* (1985) Appendix A pp. 367ff.

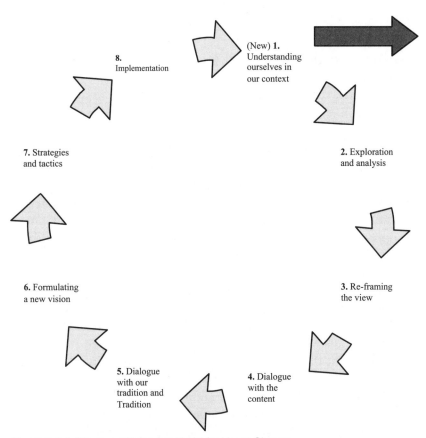

Figure 5:3 A Structured Reflection Model for Linear Change

to manage, its methodology has a great deal to commend it. Such gathering of data will lead to the next stage.

EXPLORATION AND ANALYSIS

What does all this mean? The congregation may ask critical questions of itself and of the context in which it is situated. What issues must it face? How ready is the Church for change and what kind of change should that be? What are the signs of the times and how should they be interpreted? The report acknowledges that this may be disturbing:

> Inevitably deep questions will arise about the nature and purpose of the Church and the meaning of the Christian Gospel. People should be encouraged to face

them, even if there is disagreement, as long as the discussion leads to action, and is not an evasion of it.[4]

A key role of leadership here will be to model courage and openness to what has arisen.

RE-FRAMING THE VIEW

A problem or situation can be viewed in a number of different ways, which may reveal possibilities that have hitherto gone unnoticed. This will involve thinking outside the box and laterally. It may involve asking the questions in different ways or asking very different questions. Is the glass half empty or half full? Have we a problem or an opportunity? Here is an opportunity for leadership from those whose gifts may be to turn a problem on its head, so that it can be viewed from a new angle.

Like putting a painting in a new position or in a different frame, possibilities may dawn which were not apparent before. Familiarity can lead to a form of blindness or to claims that a particular path to follow is impossible. Learning to see differently or even to see at all is an important theme of the Fourth Gospel (especially Jn 9) as well as in Luke 4.18 where Jesus quotes Isaiah in speaking of the 'recovery of sight to the blind'. Good leadership speaks of vision, but for that to be internalized by those who follow, there is a need to *give sight* and develop *insight*. 'We can't, can we?' needs to be turned into 'Why not?'

DIALOGUE WITH THE CONTEXT

The church community then needs to engage in conversation with its context to see what can be learnt from it and how it may make a contribution to it but also receive insights from the wider community. This must involve some gathering of data and views from those outside who may have a different view of what the Church is or who it is for. Key institutions or people in a locality can act as a *critical friend* of the Church and offer unique insights which should be listened to. Here the theological stance of a church and its leadership will be important. Being in the world but not of it, seeing the role of the Church as *leaven* or *salt* means interacting with the context, learning from it as well as offering it the insights of the Gospel. *The Faith in*

[4] Ibid. p. 372.

the City report calls this 'working for and with our neighbour in the community'.[5] Dialogue does not mean the abandonment of prophetic proclamation, but this needs to be balanced by a willingness to be a listening servant also, open to receive truth from whatever its source.

DIALOGUE WITH OUR TRADITION AND WITH TRADITION

Here the Church community needs to be in touch with its own history, tradition and the wider tradition of the Church. It will mean re-visiting the *wells of wisdom* that should inform Christian decision-making. Tradition, however, is not the same as precedent, though often confused with it. Tradition is the experience of the Gospel as lived through history and reflected on by the Church. In this sense it is rather like DNA in an individual, which is both unique to that person but also vitally connected to others. It will be through this exercise that the criteria for identifying authentic from inauthentic change will become apparent. The past is there not to be replicated, but to be learnt from and to be faithful to in a way that is genuinely open to the future. Here we are in touch with the Gospel as seed rather than as script or as the basis for a play that we are writing on the basis of a plot that has already been given to us, but which is capable of various kinds of enactment.

One of the key issues here will be: what is the predominant view of what the Church is, who and what it is for. Dulles' *Models of the Church* may be found to be very helpful here and a summary and adaptation of the biblical images he explores in his book is given as an Appendix.[6] None of these images are exclusive but an important issue will be which of them need to be emphasized in the light of what has been discovered by the process outlined above. Failure to do this will usually lead to adopting the Church as institution as a kind of default position with more emphasis on maintenance than on mission. Here the role of the presidential leadership in guiding and facilitating an adult understanding of the Christian faith will be important. Effective dialogue with the tradition of the Church and its scriptural base can only happen in a teaching and learning church where the formation of its members is seen to be of fundamental importance.

[5] Ibid. p. 68.
[6] Dulles, A. (2nd edn).

FORMULATING A NEW VISION

Out of this exercise a new or more vital vision for the community may emerge which needs to be expressed in ways that engage and animate the energies of all. The Christian Church has complex and multi-faceted purposes, serving the needs of its members as well as reaching out to the world in which it is. A great deal of discussion is needed about how the Church fulfils these purposes in identifiable ways in a given locale, at this particular time and in the foreseeable future. It is not sufficient to have vague aspirations or to be content with mere generalizations or to hark back nostalgically to a supposed golden age in the past. A congregation needs to have realizable goals that are specific, measurable, time limited in some way, and owned by all as well as more open aims.

Leadership with a vision is about moving to a better future, and the perfection of humans both as individuals and as a society. It is, in other words, about trying to make a difference that has the Gospel as its frame of reference. This needs to be articulated and symbolized in ways that are readily communicable. Handy notes that this is a key leadership role: 'A leader shapes and shares a vision which gives point to the work of others.' In other words, a key function is to help people see what they are doing or are being asked to do as meaningful and purposeful and how what they do may contribute to the overall purpose. It is important to note here that he does not say *originate* as if a vision was simply something to be handed down, for it is grown and contributed to by as many people as possible and then turned into feasible action. The symbolic leader holds this vision, embodies it, represents it and helps to ground it. He or she holds it up before the people so that it becomes embodied in their lives.

STRATEGIES AND TACTICS

For this to work, concrete ways forward have to be identified, which means thinking in three time frames: the present, the future and the interim process of getting there. It also means keeping the different features of change in balance.

Implementation

Not only do the strategies and tactics have to be determined but they must be organized, carried through and evaluated. This can be a difficult issue precisely because churches consist largely of people who are volunteers. Most of the literature on leadership emphasizes the importance of being able to differentiate between task needs, group maintenance needs and individual needs and that equipoise is needed here.[7] Emphasis on what is required to accomplish a task can eclipse the need to keep everyone together and resource the congregation as a group or the ability to respond to the individual, but it is equally possible to be so engaged with group or individual maintenance as to make any change almost impossible. It is all a question of balance and working collaboratively.

Three factors in linear change thus become important: (i) knowing with some degree of accuracy what the present situation is; (ii) envisioning the future in such a way as to maximize commitment to it; and (iii) devising effective means to move forward. This can be mapped in terms of time frames (Figure 5:4).

WILD OR CHAOS CHANGE

As has been noted above, this kind of change (Figure 5:5) comes about either because of some event which is beyond our control or when it is not obvious or clear what the ways forward may be. After a time, as these do emerge, planned change then begins to become possible. This situation can be compared to what happens when a sudden death leaves family not only bereaved but with considerable uncertainty as to how they are going to cope. The first step is simply about coming to terms with what has happened and working that through. This kind of change which starts with a bereavement can and often is experienced by groups also as a new situation is forced upon them.

Charles Handy, however, in his entertaining and shrewd book *Gods of Management*[8] points out that there is another factor that the leadership of any organization needs to take into account, not least when considering change, and that is its culture. Having the right culture is important for the leadership of any change. A congregation that has this right will better survive the turbulence of chaos change than one that hasn't.

Because it is composed of human beings living in varying contexts, churches will have their own way of doing things, their own style and ethos, which vary considerably one from another. This we call

---

[7]   Adair, J. (1983) *Effective Leadership.* London: Pan Macmillan.
[8]   Handy, C. (1985) *Gods of Management.* London: Souvenir Press Ltd.

Planned or linear change	Present (Situation: facts/ analysis)	Future (Vision/imagining)	Change process (Tactics)
Operation (What?)	What we do now. Mapping where we are and what we currently do. This needs to be as complete as possible a picture of activities and resources of the Church	Sets out how we envisage ourselves in the future. What will be our mission and objectives in the new situation? What will be our main activities? What will be our accepted theology and our ecclesi-ology-in-practice?	What are we going to do to move from the present to the future? What strategies for involving people in the change will there be? What will be the stages of change? How long a period for each? How will it be led and managed?
Organization (How?)	This needs to map out how we do things and thus must cover issues like climate, culture and values. What are our priorities now as a church?	How do we want to do things in future? What kind of culture and climate do we want to develop? What will our values be and how will they differ to those we hold at present? What will our priorities be? What will be our accepted theology and ecclesiology?	What do we need to change first? How will we do this? What will be the style of leadership needed to make all this happen? How will we manage continuity as well as the disjunction between past, present and future? What leadership issues are there? Reflective theology.
People (Who?)	What strengths, gifts and talents do we have now and how are they used? Who do we use? Whose capabilities are not being used? Why not?	How do we grow people and nurture what they have and who they are? How can we become more of a learning church? What will be our priorities here? Who do we need to grow?	Who will we need to support and guide people through this process to help them to feel that it is theirs? Modelling positive change and handling ambiguity. Who will be key here?

Figure 5:4 Three Time Frames and Three Factors in Linear Change

their 'culture' which may or may not be appropriate at any one time depending on a number of variables.

Handy has identified four main *cultures*, each with their own advantages and disadvantages. Sometimes an organization will have more than one culture within it which may explain some forms of conflict when they relate to each other. These are named after four

> *This can be compared with the stages that a person often undergoes after a bereavement or perhaps suddenly being made redundant or experiencing a catastrophe of some kind.*
>
> **Shock** – Feelings of being overwhelmed, frozen into immobility, caught in the headlights.
>
> **Non-acceptance** – Behaving as if it never happened as if everything was normal. Where's the problem? What problem? It will go away.
>
> **Feeling inadequate and unable to cope** – Frustration, depression, feelings of almost total inadequacy and hopelessness. We can't do this.
>
> **Coming to terms with the new situation** – The beginning of acceptance of what has happened. Letting go of the past and dawning of realism. OK. This is how it is.
>
> **Beginning to do it differently** – Trying new things out and learning from mistakes. Let's see if this works.
>
> **A new rationale** – We are beginning now to see what it is all about. New patterns emerge and become more normal. A process of making sense of what has happened.
>
> **Getting it together** – New ways of being and doing get bedded in so that the congregation say: This is how we do it now.

Figure 5:5 The Process of Wild or Chaos Change

Greek gods: *Zeus, Apollo, Athena* and *Dionysus*. He chose these images because, as he says:

> To the Greeks, religion was more a mater of custom than a formal theology. Their gods stood for certain things and, to a degree, you chose your god because you shared the values and interest which they represented.[9]

Zeus is the king of the gods and is a very personal god who has the habit of intervening directly in affairs by a shower of gold or thunderbolts. This is because the organization depends very closely on the head or founder. He or she would do everything personally if they could. Thus the organization is really an extension of its head. While it is flexible it is not very democratic. Everything depends on the competence of the leader. Without the leader the organization is dead. With an incompetent one, it is in serious trouble. Such an organization may be exciting to work in but there is a tendency to be inconsistent and arbitrary in behaviour.

Apollo is the god of harmony, rules and order. This organization has very clear structures, roles and fairly formal lines of communication. Individuals are fitted into the structure which is logical with set rules, routines and checks. However, this kind of structure finds it

---

[9] Ibid. Introduction p. 9.

difficult to cope with change or new challenges because the rule book has to be rewritten and new structures devised which can take time and a lot of effort.

Athena is the goddess of war and of the task force, good at solving problems with a warm and friendly culture which constantly responds to new challenges. It tends to be made up of co-operative colleagues working without much hierarchy and very flexibly with a minimum of standard procedures. It is a questioning culture which is fairly democratic, but is expensive in terms of time and so is not good for routine tasks.

Dionysus is an individualist culture, which puts the individual firmly in control and makes the organization resource him or her. It works best where the talents of people are what matters and the problems or tasks are such that can be best coped with by one person. Dionysians resist any form of management and have to be persuaded, cajoled, flattered and influenced to do anything together. Not a cooperative culture except where self-interest is also served.

While inevitably the personality of the leader(s) will be a factor in determining which culture or style predominates in a church, it is better that the culture is chosen in the light of perceived needs or objectives that it has. Thus an inappropriate culture can lead to many problems and conflicts that might otherwise have been avoided and this can sabotage change. All organizations will be something of a mix of these cultures but it is likely that some parts will be predominantly one of these and there will also be one which may be more overarching than the others.

Handy points out[10] that voluntary organizations, of which churches are a prime example, tend to be one of three types or a mix of them all: fellowship, service and campaigning. Fellowship organizations often move into service ones, he suggests, while others are predominantly founded to conduct some kind of campaign or fight for a cause. Each of these will need a different blend of the gods[11]. The equivalent in Christian terms are worship, ministry and prophecy which are really three different organizations under one umbrella. However, he notes that one 'god' tends to triumph over the others, so that some of the tasks get neglected. Churches are thus multifaceted

---

[10] Ibid. pp. 124ff.

[11] Anyone unhappy with Handy's pagan metaphors might try substituting religious orders, e.g. The Benedictines (fellowship/community), the Dominicans (campaigning), the Jesuits (ordered service), the early Franciscans (the free spirits?)

and each of these facets is connected to the others. Predominantly prophetic churches tend to be movements rather than organizations and thus prefer a Zeus-like figure as leader, who may neglect other aspects of the Church's life. A collaborative leadership which encompasses these three aspects must this be one option to be explored. However, voluntary organizations are often impatient of bureaucracy and therefore resistant to an Apollonian culture that can become an end in itself, but we know that some of the mistakes of the past are due to a lack of sound procedures and structures. Without them change can become mindless chaos, but too much of this culture may inhibit the very spirit that makes the organization worth belonging to. It is all a question of balance.

Voluntary bodies may have some paid employees but the majority of helpers offer their time free of remuneration. This can bring its own problems and may make leadership in change more difficult since discontent with the direction in which a church may be going can simply be demonstrated by people going elsewhere. Handy notes also that there may be some confusion in the minds of members of the congregation or, indeed, all of them, as to whether they are *customers* or *fellow workers*. Increasingly the Christian churches are trying to see their members as 'co-workers' in Christ as was explored in Chapter four and will be explored further in a later chapter. The traditional passive role for the laity is a by-product of clericalism, actively promoted by a view of the ordained person as the *doers of ministry*.

Laypeople in this category may simply respond to change by saying, 'well, you do it, then'. Leadership in change in today's church has to tackle this assumption through education and formation, not by seeing this as a way of dealing with the (temporary) problem of a shortage of clergy, but by helping church members to see that a participative in ministry church is intrinsic to what it means to be a member of the Body of Christ. Of course, it remains true that everyone, including the pastors and leaders, need to be ministered to also. Clericalism prevents ministry and care to the clergy from the laity as well as a patronizing view of laypeople which only serves to infantilize them.

Many factors have to be kept in mind when leading in change for it is a very good example of *see, judge, act*. Seeing where the Church is in its life and history in terms of people, culture, norms and assumptions; judging how best to go forward on the basis of accurate diagnosis of all the issues and problems and then doing the right things in the right way and at the right time. 'Fail to prepare, prepare to fail' is an often quoted adage. While it may be true that in one sense it is difficult to prepare for chaos change, in other ways it can be done by cultivating the right culture, spirit and ways of being that enable a positive response to the unexpected. It can often bring out the best in people although not to be attempted lightly! Keeping all change well earthed in the Gospel is, of course, the primary task of any church leader but can easily be forgotten in the rush to keep all the plates spinning.

QUESTIONS

- How apt is the suggestion that the Church needs to recognize that it is faced with chaos change?
- How useful are the ideas about *open* and *closed* systems as applied to a church?
- Is the predominant culture of the Church best suited for change today? What needs to be different?
- How can Church leaders be better prepared for leadership in change?
- Newman sees change as necessary for perfection, Belloc as a series of lesser *deaths*. Is there truth in both these statements?

Chapter 6

RE-MEMBERING THE LAITY

Although for many years the Church has professed an enthusiasm to involve, work with and utilize lay people in its ministry, when this profession is observed in practice what emerges is a very spasmodic and patchy picture of lay involvement. In some places lay people are hardly visible, save for Sunday worship when they inhabit some of the pews. Yet, in other places they take not only a full part in the exercise of ministry, but also become leaders in some areas of pastoral care, mission and liturgical activities. Why such a difference should exist is not a straightforward enquiry. Among other things, this depends on the history of participation, the diversity of ministry, the style of leadership, and the expectations of the people who attend. It also depends on the focus of ministry; whether this is primarily encouraging all people to look outwards to share the Gospel in the communities of the locale and wider; whether there is a more lay-oriented ministry into which the non-ordained have adequate input; whether the congregation see the ministry and vision of the Church to be held and implemented only by their leader or shared among the whole body; whether the focus of mission and ministry is owned by the *laos* as a whole. What is necessary in all this is that lay people are truly members of the Church; not just pew fodder, not foot soldiers to be commanded, not groups, teams or working parties that are set up to fulfil the leader's ambitions, but partners in mission and ministry for the sake of the Gospel. Where this hasn't happened in churches today, then the laity needs to be re-membered, not simply remembered when all else has failed or a plan has been hatched to drive an initiative to keep leaders content, but, as members of the Body of Christ to be constantly re-membered into that corpus, and for Christ to be re-membered into the community of believers as their head. This re-membering process is something that needs to be dynamic and life giving, but it begins with a pragmatic and theological foundation.

There are two main reasons why re-membering a theology of laity would be of help to the Church through the changes it is encountering. The first is pragmatic, in that the primary role of lay people – according to many ecclesiologists, and reflected in many church reports whatever denomination they come from – is as missionaries. Indeed, for example, wherever lay people are mentioned in the Anglican report *Mission Shaped Church*, it is agreed that they are in a prime position to be missionaries. This concurs with Congar's ecclesiology in *Lay People in the Church*,[1] and the Methodist report, *Called to Love and Praise*. What is debatable is the functional relationship, in terms of mission, between lay people and clergy. In some senses this is at the nub of the problem and will be examined more closely later. Yet, the relationship between mission, lay people and clergy is unclear because the notions of church and mission are unclear. What is needed is a new mindset towards ecclesiology and missiology, indicative of the resolution of chaos change. Re-membering, as opposed to simply remembering the laity, is about giving those who have a rightful place their position, offering a new place to a theology of laity in the Church. This would mean that lay people could find a true vocation in it. Lay discipleship training will then have a focus of deepening spiritual growth alongside promoting a living witness, equipping lay people to be signs of the Kingdom in the world. The second reason is strategic in that once the role and purpose of laity is clarified, then the priesthood of the Church can be defined against it, which in turn gives greater definition to a whole ecclesiology. When this happens then a partnership of laity and clergy, engaged in ministry and mission is possible.

Newman was one of the greatest proponents of a theology of laity. In his campaign for a Catholic university, he advocated a well educated laity. Yves Congar, basing his ecclesiology on Newman's, is another theologian who promoted lay people in the Church. His aspirations included laity becoming more than those who only sit in the pews and give alms. In one sense, both theologians were acknowledging that lay people, particularly the education of the laity, was being ignored. Even in the contemporary church, lay people, who form as much as ninety-nine per cent of the membership, are again often ignored, for

---

[1] Congar, Y. *Lay People in the Church*, pp. 333–378.

example in the majority of training schemes. It is interesting to note that in the Anglican Church the vast majority of training reports over the last fifty years have concerned clergy training, not lay training,[2] a scenario which cannot continue if mission is a priority. The Church needs to reposition its theology of laity to bring a pragmatic and strategic focus to the role of lay people, to define the role of clergy, to begin to form a solid ecclesiology and to truly engage in mission.

A BRIEF HISTORY OF LAY INVOLVEMENT

Richard Hooker (1554–1600), as Paul Avis proclaims was 'unquestionably the greatest Anglican theologian'.[3] He envisaged a partnership between laity and clergy. He wanted the whole body politic to be responsible for the making of laws, and for each parish church to contain clergy and laity kneeling together at the communion rail before one Lord, with one faith, through one baptism. The place of the laity in the Reformation was complex; however, what is apparent is that the concept of laity emerged from the period with increased significance. As Avis puts it: 'Under the impress of the Reformation and its aftermath, the Church of England became – what it remains to this day – very much a layperson's church'.[4] It is a matter for debate whether the Church of England is still 'very much a layperson's church'. Thompsett highlights a contemporary debate concerning the degree to which laity are actually supported and heard today. In her essay *The Laity*, in *The Study of Anglicanism*[5] she sets out the case for a 'conviction that the ethical character of Christian witness depends upon giving priority to furthering the mission of laity in the world'.[6] Her critique rests upon a central issue that the foundational event of the Church of England, the sixteenth-century Reformation, had as its hallmarks for the general populace, 'an inclusive social vision of the commonwealth', and expansive vocational, biblical and

---

[2] For example, the latest Anglican training report 'Formation for Ministry within a Learning Church' advocates huge recommendations for clerical training, and by and large treats lay training as a pre-ordination course. *Formation for Ministry within a Learning Church*, GS 1496. (2003). London: Church House Publishing.

[3] Avis, P. (2002), *Anglicanism and the Christian Church*, (added in the revised and expanded edn). London: Continuum, p. 31.

[4] Avis, P. *Anglicanism and the Christian Church*, p. 61.

[5] Thompsett, F. H. in Sykes, et al. eds (1998 [1988]) *The Study of Anglicanism* (revised ed.). London: SPCK, pp. 277–293.

[6] Ibid. p. 272.

educational inheritances.[7] Her assertion is that by the Civil War, the laity was increasingly able to debate with clergy over the future of the Church, but that despite ninety-nine per cent of the Church being lay, lay perspectives have been 'eclipsed, underestimated or strategically ignored for long periods of the Church's history'.[8]

Hearing what the laity wants of the Church is a point made by Celia Hahn, the former Director of the American-based *Alban Institute* for lay studies:

> Much of the time, in our churches, the clergy speak and the laity listen. Those are clearly useful and appropriate activities. But I believe it is also very important for the laity to speak and for the clergy to listen ... When Elizabeth Kubler-Ross wanted to know what dying people need, she asked dying people. It would seem equally appropriate to ask lay people what they need from their churches.[9]

Paul Lakeland, in the *Liberation of the Laity* argues for a *Promethean*-type task to be laid before the laity. That is:

> The lay Christian is the one upon whom the burden and honour of working for a more fully human world have been placed. These characteristics do not make the lay Christian any more likely than the non-Christian to further the discourse of the human community towards its ends, because they provide no special insights about the particular steps that need to be taken. But they should keep the lay Christian at the table longer ... Jesus, of course is the exemplar of 'responsible commitment to the process,' though we usually call it his 'faithfulness to the Father's calling'. And so we can say that the lay vocation is responsible commitment to the process of unfolding human freedom.[10]

He also makes the point that as the mission of the Church moves in its meaning from 'saving proclamation' to 'saving praxis', the role of the clergy becomes more an ancillary role and the role of the laity predominates. There are other authors, such as Paul Stevens, Jeremy Miller, C. S. Dessain, Kenneth Hylson-Smith and David Clarke who have written extended studies of the role of the laity, but one person who has contributed extensively is the Roman Catholic author and theologian Yves Congar.

---

[7] Ibid. p. 282.

[8] Ibid. p. 278.

[9] Hahn, C. A. (1985) *Lay Voices in an Open Church*. New York: The Alban Institute, p. 3.

[10] Lakeland, P. (2004) [2002] *The Liberation of the Laity: In Search of an Accountable Church*. London: Continuum, p. 184 (emphasis in original).

CONGAR'S THEOLOGY OF LAITY

Congar's contribution to a theology of laity is immense. What he constructs, based on Newman's theology and in a Newman-like way, is a church that understands laity as exercising priestly, kingly and prophetic ministry for the world. In his portrayal of mission, the Church exists for the world (laity being *secular* in the sense of missionary), and the priesthood of the Church exists to support the laity in order to be missioners. This pragmatic emphasis is demonstrated in some of the documents of Vatican II, which contribute greatly to a theology of laity,[11] (in some ways as Carriquiry suggests, it brought it to maturity).[12] In Vatican II, the laity has a recognized calling. The calling comes directly from union with Christ as head of the Church. As a result, charisms are given. Laity has a distinctive role in the apostolic ministry through circumstances of life, family, job and leisure. In a final section of *Lumen Gentium*,[13] the perfect example of this theology of *laypersonhood* is exemplified by and through Mary,[14] who personifies a ministry of wisdom (pondering in her heart) and sacrifice (her heart was pierced).

It is relatively easy to detect the hand of Congar in the chapters of the *Apostolate of the Laity* decree,[15] and Vatican II embraces his theology, enhancing the role and ontology of the layperson. In the documents of Vatican II, lay people have a calling that is marked by a distinctly secular and spiritual quality. They are to collaborate with clergy and bishops, act as an organic body, present the Word in liturgy, catechetical activities, the care of souls, and administration; and infuse the Christian spirit in the local, national and international arenas.

[11] However, note that this was not without frustration and difficulty. For an account of the changes and trajectories of the various views of the laity in Vatican II see Klostermann, F. (1969) in *Commentary On the Documents of Vatican II*, ed. by Herbert Vorgrimler, trans. by W. Glen-depel, and others, Vol. 3. London: Burns and Oates, pp. 273–404.

[12] Carriquiry, G. in Apostola, N. (ed.) (1998) *A Letter from Christ to the World.* Geneva: WCC Publications, pp. 107–113.

[13] Ibid. p. 94ff.

[14] *The Documents of Vatican II*, ed. by Abbott, W. M. (1966), London: Geoffrey Chapman, pp. 589ff.

[15] Ibid. Apostolicam Actuositatem p. 489.

He writes that lay people have for too long been subordinate in the Church, kneeling before the altar and sitting in the pew.[16] They need to become fully part of the Church, even defining the role of clergy:

> May we not be on the eve of a new spring, a vigil of Pentecost? The demands of a laity awakening to consciousness of its place and responsibilities in the Church already give us clergy some inkling of what the welcoming, the cultivation and ripening of such crops will call for from us.[17]

Congar was clearly prophetic in his assessment of the laity and this has a direct spin-off for the clergy. Seeing lay people as subjects, the clergy then take their supportive role of enabling mission. Vatican II spells this out further when it directs the whole church, working together, to construct a temporal order directed to God through Christ. Groups need to unite their efforts by pooling their resources, with hierarchy promoting and supporting the projects, and dioceses specifically set up through councils to assist lay activity. Notwithstanding the subsequent failure of Vatican II to live up to its expectations and despite attempts to spell out the co-responsibility of laity, deacons, priests and bishops, the theology of laity promulgated at the Council was astonishing. *Lumen Gentium* demonstrated a reshaping of ecclesiology even in its location of the section concerning the *People of God* immediately after the opening *Mystery of the Church*, and particularly before the chapter on hierarchical structure. This confirmed how far the Roman Church had travelled from Vatican I. It is also notable for its famous ending in the rehearsal of Mariology.

Congar's missiology embraces reconciliation of the world to God, demonstrated in his diagrammatic representation of the laity's part in the Church's priestly function.[18] However, Lakeland cites this as one of the main causes for the crisis of identity among the clergy in the post-conciliar period.[19] He suggests that although the theology and event of Vatican II were exciting, the voices were to some extent silenced by Congar's radical views on priesthood, which saw both lay and clerical priests operative in church and world.

Yet the voice of the laity needs to be heard, for as Congar believed, the Church exists 'in the meeting and harmonising of hierarchical

---

[16] Congar, Y. *Lay People in the Church.* p. xxiii.

[17] Ibid. p. xxxi.

[18] Ibid. pp. 181–183.

[19] Lakeland, P. *The Liberation of the Laity,* p. 55.

communication from above, and a community's (sic) consent'.[20] This consent can only be given if the voice of the community, not just the individual, is heard. Democratization, that sees the Church making its decisions through one person with one vote, cannot apply here. Laity is the *pleroma* of the hierarchical priesthood[21] and its missionary responsibility is kenotic – to go to the lowest place in order to begin to scale the heights.

THE MISSION AND MINISTRY OF THE WHOLE CHURCH

As has been said earlier, various approaches towards involving the laity more in the exercise of mission and ministry from different denominational stances have been written. *Called to Love and Praise* and *The Sign we Give* are but two. Another, which commends itself from the Anglican tradition, is to be found in a report that took some seven or eight years to write. In the summer of 2007 a report was published which was surprising in terms of both its timing (after the reports on training and mission had been written) and the clarity it offered. The full title of the report is *The Mission and Ministry of the Whole Church: Biblical, Theological and Contemporary Perspectives* (known from here as MMWC). It was produced by the Faith and Order Advisory Group, approved by the House of Bishops and circulated in the General Synod in 2007. In 2001, the General Synod debated a report *For Such a Time as This: A Renewed Diaconate in the Church of England*. This report was referred back to the authors for further work, 'seeking to relate ordained and lay forms of ministry to each other'.[22] The group, including Paul Avis, Paula Gooder, Robert Hannaford, Vernon White and Martin Davie spent six years (2001–2007) in the formation of the response.

The report makes a number of very good points about ministry and mission, which would have informed and increased the likelihood of a more effective outcome of previous training and mission reports in the Anglican Church. For example in terms of mission, it examined British cultural life, using the analysis from *Mission Shaped Church*, and

[20] A point made by Paul Lakeland in *The Liberation of the Laity*, p. 56 from Yves Congar, *Lay People in the Church*, p. 250. (p. 263 in the edition from which Lakeland worked).

[21] Congar, Y. *Lay People in the Church*, p. 313.

[22] *The Mission and Ministry of the Whole Church: Biblical, Theological and Contemporary Perspectives*, (2007) GS misc. 854, The Archbishops' Council. London: The General Synod of the Church of England, p. vii.

supplemented this with Grace Davie's work on vicarious religion. It concluded with four points of missionary consensus:

- that Christian truths need to be 'embodied in a plausible fashion in the life of the Christian community'
- that each congregation should become what Lesslie Newbigin calls a 'hermeneutic of the Gospel'
- that 'new forms of Christian mission communities (*fresh expressions*), relevant to people today, are formed'
- that ecumenism is made integral to mission.

These focuses are no easy task for any local church, yet they are crucial for the success of its work and the deployment of its leaders. Leaders are called to lead the hermeneutical process in order that the Church can find its relevance to the communities it serves. However, the leader in such a situation must work closely with lay people, as it is they who also have direct knowledge of the local and wider communities. A re-membering of the laity in hermeneutical terms means giving authority to lay people to speak about and reflect on their experience of how things are. As Hahn said earlier, leaders need to listen in order to enable the hermeneutical process.

Another significant word in the bullet points above is *plausible*. Christian truths need to be 'embodied in a plausible fashion in the life of the Christian community'. Too often becoming and remaining a member of the Body of Christ means taking on the personal constructs of the local church. In other words, inhabiting the patterns of a set order of behaviour and belief in order to belong. When someone joins up and critiques the way things are done, it can be a matter of real dissonance, in terms of conduct and cognitive understanding. When a new person joins a team, the team is new. This is often quoted but rarely taken note of in church teams. When someone new joins, it is not just a question of inducting them, it is also important to induct the new team altogether. The individual will need to know where things are, how things are done and what to do in certain situations, and so on. But, it is equally important that the team adjusts and incorporates (literally becomes a new body) the new member. Re-membering the laity means constantly being renewed and its subsequent hermeneutical process will need that plausibility, honesty and courage which enables it to be dynamic. The alternative inertia derived from a non-hermeneutical process produces out of date behaviours and beliefs, stagnation of activity through loss of meaning and the eventual abandonment of the project altogether.

The way this re-membering process might begin will be explored later, but its sustainability will depend on checking how much the Church is in touch with reality, adjusting the way it conducts itself, and comparing the form of emerging ecclesiology with the theological principles outlined earlier here in Chapter 2. In terms of this third point, the MMWC report offers a further, and perhaps more shorthand way of encouraging good re-membering.

The report summarizes ordained and lay appropriation of the threefold identity that Newman, and before him Calvin had advocated:

> Because Christians are made to share in Christ's threefold messianic identity, the diaconate points to the *prophetic* nature of the Church, her calling to convey the word of God to those who are meant to hear it. The presbyterate points to the *priestly* nature of the Church, her reconciling ministry through the authoritative word of forgiveness or blessing and through the sacraments as a whole. The episcopate points to the *pastoral* nature of the Church, guiding, leading, shepherding the flock of Christ. Ordained ministries embody and proclaim for all to see what is true of the whole body. Lay ministries participate in this reality according to their calling. All the faithful are marked by baptism and share in the messianic identity of Jesus as Prophet, Priest and King, an identity that he imparts to his Church because it is his Body and one with him.[23]

It is interesting to note how the work of Newman is being interpreted here. On the surface, the threefold identity is applied to the ordained ministry and left loosely and vaguely defined in terms of lay ministers. Yet, not uncontrovertibly, Newman recognized lay ministry in terms of the priestly office. Was Newman making a theological or cultural point in his location of laity as part of the priestly office? What he did not mean was that lay people were priests in the same way that ordained priests are – they are different. We might express this difference today as lay people being priests of the world and the ordained as priests of the Church. The marginalization of the laity is a failure in acknowledging their participation in Christ, which also diminishes the ordained priesthood. That may be a question to be considered in another place, but the reality of the situation today is that re-membering the laity means enabling lay people to be prophetic, in the sense of having studied theology at whatever level and then to be able to articulate that in the public domain, to be priestly in devotion and worship and private prayer, being partnered by the ordained in seeking to do this, and to be kingly by exercising authority and pastoral care in the world. With regard to this last role,

---

[23] *The Mission and Ministry of the Whole Church*, p. 72 (emphasis in original).

Stephen Sykes produced a very helpful book on power and authority,[24] which towards the end advocates a process of handling these tricky issues based on Gregory the Great's *Liber Regalae Pastoralis*, a pastoral rule which he sent to Britain with Augustine in the early seventh century. Exercising kingly rule and authority and power in this context means disposing power with great care so as to derive from it what is profitable and subdue its temptations towards pride and abuse. Re-membering the laity is about giving due emphasis to the three offices and the different ways in which the ontological ordained leadership fulfils this.

How can this ambition be achieved?

There is much literature written about how collaborative ministry might work in practical ways including the laity. It is the purpose here to offer theological insights from which practical issues can be addressed. When suggesting a church re-members its laity, a theological starting point must be in Jesus' command in the Passover meal 'do this in remembrance of me', sometimes known as an anamnetic statement. Macquarrie shows how the four biblical narratives of the last supper, in the Synoptic Gospels and 1 Corinthians, vary in their emphasis.[25] The anamnetic nature of church, asserting the death of Christ as an act of remembrance is to be found in 1 Corinthians and Luke, but eschatological emphases are in all four. The remembrance perspective of the texts and looking forward to the Kingdom meal in heaven is a highly inclusive model in temporal terms. The significance of looking back and forward at the same time is also highly important. Sometimes, and in some denominations one or other of the perspectives is omitted and the Orthodox theologian John Zizioulas recognizes a problem for ecclesiology here. He explains:

> The identification of the Church's ministry with that of Christ is to be seen in existential *soteriological* terms which have profound anthropological and cosmological implications. If soteriology means, as it was the case in the patristic period, not so much a juridical reality by means of which forgiveness is granted for an act of disobedience, but rather a realization of *theosis*, as communion of man – and through him of creation – in the very life of the Trinity then this identification acquires existential importance.[26]

[24] Sykes, S. (2006) *Power and Christian Theology*.
[25] Macquarrie, J. (1997) *A Guide to the Sacraments*, pp. 101–156.
[26] Zizioulas, J. D. *Being As Communion*, p. 211 (emphasis in original).

In order to achieve not just a functional collaboration in ministry, which might only encompass a group of individuals working together, but an ontologistic collaborative ministry where the participants realize their essential communion, Eucharistic theology needs to retain its eschatological identity. Sometimes churches adopt a reductionist view which demonstrates a juridical reality, signified in historical sacramental theology (Jesus' sacrificial death), but the sense of communion, as in the life of the Trinity is lost if the eschatological view is abandoned. What this means is that in a Eucharistic context a remembered laity is a laity that has gained forgiveness for acts of disobedience, but a re-membered laity is one that is in communion with the very heart of the Trinity.

Putting all this in another way, the re-membered post Easter and Pentecost church needs to be indicative not only of Christology but also pneumatology. If the re-membering is only suggestive of Christology, and pneumatology is all but lost, the view of the ordained in a theology of priesthood becomes exclusive. Also, the priesthood of believers is concealed, and a picture begins to emerge of an ecclesiology that is set in a model of the individual ordained minister as the head of the Church. Alternatively, a sacramental theology of laity predicated on the Spirit in the Church and marked by communion is essentially an eschatological expression of *ecclesia*. It is plural, relational and charismatic. By not developing it, several dangers ensue: the threat of a controlling leadership, a lack of a basis for mission, a priesthood without a people, the destruction of the nature of priesthood itself. Not only is a sacramental view of laity damaged, but in consequence, so is the view of Christology. To take a low view of laity means to take a low view of incarnation. Congar combines his high view of incarnational theology with a high view of laity. He says:

> Lay people are called to the same end as clergy or monks – to the enjoyment of our inheritance as sons of God; but they have to pursue and attain this end without cutting down their involvement in the activities of the world, in the realities of the primal creation, in the disappointments, the achievements, the stuff of history. The laity is called to God's work in the world.[27]

A sacramental theology of laity enables lay people to be signs of the Kingdom, priests to the world. A lack of it creates a clerical caste, which skews Christology and Trinitarian theology. Zizioulas warns of

---

[27] Congar, Y. *Lay People in the Church*, p. 16.

the danger of creating two autonomies when talking about ministry.[28] The first is to separate ministry and ordination, (and in this he means the ordination of all believers) and the second is to treat Christology apart from Trinitarian theology. He says, 'this gives rise to Christomonistic tendencies in understanding the person and ministry of Christ and ... to great difficulties in relating the Church's ministry to that of Christ'. Christomonism is the overemphasis of Christology, such that pneumatology is absent, or degraded to such an extent that the Trinity becomes a hierarchy of authority, rather than a differentiation by specificity of relationship. For Zizioulas, 'the identification of the Church's ministry with that of Christ is possible only if we let our *Christology be conditioned pneumatologically', He* outlines how the term *vicar* often means the representation of someone who is absent, while its correct meaning can only be biblically defined in the sense of representation by participation.[29] A lack of pneumatology, the over and almost exclusive emphasis on the clergy as the central focus of ministry, and the lack of attention to the participation of laity will strongly suggest a Christomonistic tendency.

To combat the heretical tendency of some churches towards Christomonism some principles need to be considered. Christomonism tends to reveal itself in the visible church, especially in structural terms, in an exclusively one-man ministry. The heresy behind this is the model of Christ as a singular human entity in his incarnational ministry. The sending of the Spirit at Pentecost not only equipped the Church but also removed the impression of a *one-man* appearance of Christ, and replaced it with Christ's spirit in all. The model of a one-man ministry cannot be justified in the light of the Spirit, but it is not altogether easy to rectify the situation if it has arisen. In order to move from a Christomonistic to a Trinitarian ecclesiology a number of actions are needed. An inherent hubrism, which puts the leader on a pedestal needs to be remedied. The psychology of hubrism is complex and can take time to adjust. The twenty-first century is marked by a celebrity culture and it might be tempting for the celebrant to seek to become the celebrity. When congregations idolize their leader then the leader can be prone to believe the press and step onto the plinth. Stepping off it is much more challenging and sometimes will require specialist support. Some sections of the

---

[28] Zizioulas, J. D. *Being As Communion*, p. 209.
[29] Ibid. p. 230.

Church now provide work-based learning groups or other such opportunities to explore these kinds of issues.

Structural and organizational phenomena also need addressing to enable the leader to move hegemonic positions within the shape of the Church. To use the model offered earlier, moving around the tambourine can be costly, and sometimes seem impossible because of the structures. For example, leaders can be so gathered up in the running of the Church, they never have time to move out of it resulting in a closeted hegemonic ecclesiastical life. Leaders need to exercise their giftedness, not just within the tambourine, but outside it as well, just as every disciple and minister exercise their ministerial roles, and this will require cutting through structural barriers. It will also become at times the sacrificial role of leadership to make straight the path for members to exercise their ministry.

However, in a church where Christomonism has already made its mark, it is quite likely that lay people have become the Cinderella of attention in terms of being truly involved in the Church's ministry and mission. Even though they may secretly believe quite different things to what they have been told from the pulpit, in the light of not being very active they are likely to leave the clergy to do the thinking and ministry. They may be expected to give and support but not to advise or offer opinion. Newman realized this problem in his day and because of his views was attacked in this famous quotation by Mgr Talbot, who asked:

> What is the province of the laity? To hunt, to shoot, to entertain? These matters they understand, but to meddle with ecclesiastical matters they have no right at all . Dr Newman is the most dangerous man in England, and you will see that he will make use of the laity against your Grace.

Conclusion

What is key here is the emphasis on lay people being re-membered. This derives its importance from Christ's words of institution by which he did not only mean that we should remember his presence through bread and wine, but be re-membered by it. Thus we commune with the Spirit, Christ and the Father and have our ecclesiology shaped by a Trinitarian doctrine of church. Further, lay people become the missionaries of the Church. Nevertheless, often what happens is that for a variety of reasons lay people take up and maintain positions of guardians of the Church rather than signposts to it. The effect is to burden the laity with maintenance and leave mission devoid of resource. MMWC, along with other reports, attempts to unravel this dichotomy and offers a renewed understanding of the missionary project. This position has its roots in Congar and Newman and in the metaphor of Prophet, Priest and King. Yet, to remedy the lack of mission activity in many churches in the West, as shall be seen in Newman's theology, an emphasis must be placed on the education and encouragement of the laity, the competence of the clergy to enable lay people to fulfil their vocation and a willingness to work together.

QUESTIONS

- What are the costs and benefits of promoting a theology of laity in the Church today?
- How can a church guard against Christomonism?
- How is the work of the Spirit exemplified in your church and who is involved in this?
- What do you think are the consequences of re-membering the laity?

Chapter 7

BREATHING TOGETHER: LAITY AND CLERGY DOING THEOLOGY AND MISSION

To truly re-member the laity means much hard work by both the laity and leaders of the Church. In so doing, this will likely beg the question as to what kind of relationship is fostered between the leadership and membership of the Church? Although, in general terms, progress towards a less clerically maintained church has been made in some quarters over the past century, with church councils, and wider consultations, there is still further work to be done. Newman also faced this in his day. In the Church he served two problems existed to make the challenge hard. First there was a high degree of clericalism among the clergy, demonstrated by Talbot's phrases quoted in the last chapter. Second, at least at the beginning of the time of the Oxford Movement, ordination was somewhat of a default for those who left university with no specific vocation and in need of a living somewhere. This meant that clergy had little understanding of their vocation, indeed of vocation in general. The resistance to laity taking a full part in the ministry of the Church might continue to irritate the twenty-first century church, but perhaps it isn't as vehement as in Newman's time. Yet it is interesting that Newman never sought to teach in a seminary, to influence the clergy of the time. Perhaps he might have succeeded more in his ambitions for a distinctive ecclesiology if he had. Nevertheless, his concern was to enable the laity to mobilize and be the Church.

In the 1850s he was given a chance to make a substantial impact on the vocation and education of the laity. He was invited by the Catholic bishops to begin a university in Dublin for Catholic lay people who were barred from attending Oxford and Cambridge because of a requirement to assent to the Anglican Thirty-nine Articles. Before he started the project he wrote a masterful series of lectures on education outlining what we can only regard today as one of the best, perhaps the best theology of education ever written. The series was edited and combined into a volume entitled *The Idea of a University*. In this he set out the purposes, goals and methods of education and in particular of liberal education. It must be remembered that he lived in a very utilitarian world where education was largely only valued if it enabled progress. It might be agreed that education is best when it is useful, but when education becomes the slave of the economy, industry and commerce it quite often fails to enrich the individual or community. And those who control it tend to care less for the 'softer' subjects such as literature, the arts and indeed religion. His encouragement in these Dublin lectures was towards a more enriching, truly enlightening and enhancing liberal education – an education that was freeing, focused and persuasive. He described it as:

> the education which gives a man a clear conscious view of his own opinions and judgements, a truth in developing them, an eloquence in expressing them, and a force in urging them.[1]

He wasn't trying to cram people with facts, rather, to educate the head and heart and conscience. The Irish university project concluded for Newman rather unsuccessfully when he returned to Birmingham in 1858 due to political problems regarding staffing, but his ambition for the role and place of lay people did not wane. Shortly after returning he became involved in what has become known as the *Rambler* affair, after the periodical bearing the name. An article of his was published in the journal under the title *On Consulting the Faithful in Matters of Doctrine* (July 1859) (referred to as *OCF* from here) and was later summarized in an appended portion of *The Arians of the Fourth Century*. Jean Guitton surmises that the article 'leads one to reflect about the work of the Holy Ghost in the Church through a faithful laity'.[2]

OCF was Newman's most explicit work on the laity. In this he showed that it is the vital responsibility of leaders of the Church to consult the laity in a very particular way. He said that at one time in the Church's history it was the laity that saved the Church from heresy not the hierarchy. It was the faithful who had led the Church. He showed how the laity has the capacity to guide and direct the

---

[1] *Idea*, pp. 177–178.
[2] Guitton, J. (1964) *The Church and the Laity: From Newman to Vatican II* trans. by Malachy Gerard Carroll, Alba House, New York, p. 11.

Church even in matters of doctrine. They can form and lead the Church's direction and belief. Because of this it is crucial that at any time they should be consulted. And he defined the consultation like this:

> we talk of 'consulting our barometer' about the weather – the barometer only attests the fact of the state of the atmosphere. In like manner, we may consult a watch or a sun-dial about the time of day. A physician consults the pulse of his patient; but not in the same sense in which his patient consults him.[3]

Sometimes in church life the laity, as the Body of Christ, comes to an intuitive consensus about an issue – maybe women priests, or the ordering of worship, or a need in the world. It is not a coup, nor a sleight against the clergy, it is simply a view that has weight. It is the common sense of the people, and Newman believed it to be crucial to the Church's development. When the faithful, in their consensus demonstrate this, he believed and proclaimed that what they say should be noted carefully – what he called *consulted* – and in taking this stance he entered the debate about authority which still rages today. But he went further and asked what then is the role of leaders? He believed they were to be faithful and servant like, pastors, teachers and discerners, teaching the faith, listening to views, weighing up, assessing, reflecting, thinking and probing more deeply. In this way he longed for a partnership to emerge between clergy and laity, which he described as *conspiratio* – breathing together.

His views provoked the famous quotation of Msgr Talbot, quoted earlier, but Newman had no time for this attitude and said:

> I want a laity, not arrogant, not rash in speech, not disputatious, but men who know their religion, who enter into it, who know just where they stand, who know what they hold, and what they do not, who know their creed so well, that they can give an account of it, who know so much of history that they can defend it. I want an intelligent, well-instructed laity.[4]

He wanted lay people to be able to give reason for what they believed. He wanted clergy who would offer rich and relevant lay education. He longed for a church where the voice of the laity was heard, loud and clear.

However, there is another issue raised by the *Rambler* incident, concerning the nature of lay and clerical authority, which leads to a question about who actually does theology. With regard to this, Newman effectively repositioned the authority of lay voices when

[3] *OCF*, pp. 199.
[4] *Prepos.*, pp. 390–391.

engaged in dialogues concerning church doctrine. This was highly contentious in the Church of the time, and led to scrutiny of his theology. Concerning the specific affair that was sparked by his article in the *Rambler* Newman wrote:

> The *Rambler*, then, has these words at p. 122: 'in the preparation of a dogmatic definition, the faithful are consulted, as lately in the instance of the Immaculate Conception'. Now two questions bearing upon doctrine have been raised on this sentence, putting aside the question of fact as regards the particular instance cited, which must follow the decision on the doctrinal questions: viz. first, whether it can, with doctrinal correctness, be said that an *appeal* to the faithful is one of the preliminaries of a definition of doctrine; and second, granting that the faithful are taken into account, still, whether they can correctly be said to be *consulted*. I shall remark on both these points, and I shall begin with the second.[5]

The history of the controversy, well documented as it is, is not entirely significant here. However, the two questions that form the basis of his argument are highly relevant. First, Newman reckoned that in order to consult the laity over matters of doctrine the definition of what *consultation* meant needed to be answered. He drew a distinction between belief and judgement and suggested:

> 'In the preparation of a dogmatic definition, the faithful are consulted'. Doubtless their advice, their opinion, their judgment on the question of definition is not asked; but the matter of fact, viz. their belief, is sought for, as a testimony to that apostolic tradition, on which alone any doctrine whatsoever can be defined.[6]

In doing this Newman was appealing to the illative sense of the laity. *En masse*, the laity comes to a belief in certain propositions and this belief ought to be taken into consideration by the Holy See as part of the process of interpretation. In order to explain his thinking further, he suggested alternative phrases for *consult*, such as:

> '*regard* is had to the sense of the faithful', or, 'there is an *appeal* to the general voice of the faithful', or, '*inquiry* is made into the belief of the Christian people', or, 'the definition is not made without a previous *reference* to what the faithful will think of it and say of it,' or though any other form of words had been used, stronger or weaker, expressive of the same general idea, viz. *that the sense of the faithful is not left out of the question* by the Holy See among the preliminary acts of defining a doctrine.[7]

Lamenting how language can be misunderstood and wording can cause problems, he comes to the first question which he had asked,

---

[5] *OCF*, pp. 198–199 (emphasis in original).
[6] *On Consulting the Faithful*, introduction by John Coulson, p. 55.
[7] *OCF*, p. 200 (emphasis in original).

namely 'why the faithful should be consulted?' He has two straight-forward answers:

- Because the body of the faithful is one of the witnesses to the fact of the tradition of revealed doctrine.
- Because their consensus through Christendom is the voice of the Infallible Church.

He appeals to the Early Church to justify the first of the answers, reasoning that the tradition of the apostles manifests itself:

> Sometimes by the mouth of the episcopacy, sometimes by the doctors, sometimes by the people, sometimes by liturgies, rites, ceremonies, and customs, by events, disputes, movements, and all those other phenomena which are comprised under the name of history. It follows that none of these channels of tradition may be treated with disrespect; granting at the same time fully, that the gift of discerning, discriminating, defining, promulgating, and enforcing any portion of that tradition resides solely in the *Ecclesia docens*.[8]

The laity then, in order to be consulted, first has to be thought of as worth consulting. It needs to be listened to and respected. This leads to Newman's second answer concerning why they should be heard 'because their consensus through Christendom is the voice of the infallible Church'.

For Newman, the laity possesses a creed given it by a catechesis which is etched into its being 'as a direction of the Holy Ghost'.[9] It is an illative sense.[10] It is pre-reflective and given not by a seminary or preacher, but by an instinctual sense, guided by the Spirit. Its consent therefore, can be regarded as an individuative pneumato-logical expression, distinct but not separate from the teaching of the *pastorum*. Indeed Newman regarded the parish priest as part of the laity, giving him the dual role of both part of the hierarchy and part of the laity. However, he went one stage further in his analysis. He understood there to be two strands of tradition, episcopal (handed down from bishop to bishop) and prophetic (interpretive and breath-giving). These two strands might be regarded as a collaborative pneumatological expression. The laity is not part of the episcopal

---

[8] *OCF*, p. 205.

[9] Ibid. p. 211.

[10] For an explanation of the illative sense of the Church, see Merrigan, T. (1991) *Clear Heads and Holy Hearts: The Religious and Theological Ideal of John Henry Newman.* Louvain: Peeters Press, pp. 202–254. Merrigan explains the illative sense by means of a model of polarity first, in the individual then he applies this to *On Consulting the Faithful.*

tradition in the same way as the hierarchy, and the hierarchy is not part of the prophetic tradition in the same way as the laity. Each has its own distinct identity and contribution to the process. Terrence Merrigan makes the point:

> *Consulting the Faithful* has been described as Newman's nearest approach to a complete treatment of the laity's role (Femiano) and this is certainly true. Even here, however, Newman's essentially holistic vision persists. The fundamental insight grounding his argument in 1859 is an organic conception of the Church within which 'each constituent portion ... has its proper functions and no portion can be safely neglected,' since the 'tradition of the Apostles' is the possession of the whole body. Accordingly, 'though the laity be but the reflection or echo of the clergy in matters of faith, yet there is something in the *pastorum et fidelium conspiratio* which is not in the pastors alone'.[11]

It is when the individuative and collaborative pneumatological expressions combine that *conspiratio,* breathing together, begins. Hierarchy discerns, discriminates, defines, promulgates and enforces the tradition by consulting the laity as a matter of fact, but the revelatory process also places a primary responsibility on the illative sense of the laity. Even though the laity is not exclusively infallible in itself, (episcopacy, doctors of the Church, liturgies, rites, ceremonies and customs being other aspects of the revelatory process), the laity can be infallible when called to be, as Newman observed in the fourth century Arian controversy.

Femiano, referred to by Merrigan above, distinguishes the functions of the hierarchy with regard to faith. He contrasts Newman's view and Perrone's view, (Perrone had written on the Immaculate Conception in 1848), in their discussion concerning the roles of hierarchy and laity. He suggests that Perrone categorized the hierarchy as being the exclusive definers of doctrine, and the faithful as witnesses to tradition. However, Newman's view was that in *conspiratio,* both the hierarchy *and* the faithful act as witnesses to the faith. The separation of hierarchy and faithful in Perrone's understanding led to a separation of the processes of defining and witnessing and in turn defined hierarchy as separate from laity. Newman's combination of hierarchy and faithful in the witnessing process honours the fact that both hierarchy and faithful are part of the discerning voices of the *laos.*

Femiano continues that, although the hierarchy and faithful can find *conspiratio,* this does not mean that there is no distinction

---

[11] Merrigan, T. *Clear Heads and Holy Hearts,* pp. 236–237.

between them: 'The relations between them do not cease to be those of the *Church teaching* and the *Church that has been taught.*[12]' Yet even here, there is no final and complete distinction. Femiano concludes:

> Newman accepted and used Ullathorne's remark that the pious belief and devotion of the laity were the '*faithful reflection* of the pastoral teaching'. The faithful were not purely passive, however, for, as a person might consult a glass to learn about himself, so the bishops, consulting their 'faithful reflection' in the people, might come to know things which they could have learned in no other way. In this way, the *sensus fidelium* helps to instruct the bishops on the sentiment of the Church.[13]

Newman mounted his concept of the infallibility of the Church on the plinth of revelation. Revelation, by definition, could not err but it did need the participation of the full church and this involved the voice of the laity. His understanding of lay people as part of the expression of the infallible church reveals, according to Coulson, five characteristics of their consent:[14]

1. A testimony to apostolic dogma.
2. A *phronema* (instinct) deep in the bosom of the mystical body of Christ.
3. A direction of the Holy Spirit.
4. An answer to prayer.
5. A jealousy of error, which at once feels as a scandal.

Coulson's argument is that numbers two and five of this list are at the heart of Newman's thought. The *phronema* is a real assent to judgements of faith, and the jealousy of error is part of the foundation of his educational doctrine, giving the freedom to feel scandal and therefore discern error. Newman's understanding that the laity must be consulted is because they have a unique part in the *pastorum* and *fidelium conspiratio*, one that could be partly defined as an impression of what is right and not right. This is uniquely theirs, separate, and not necessarily held by the pastors. The faithful's instinct and devotion forms the basis of the mind of the Church before it is defined.

Chadwick illustrates this further by showing how Perrone and Newman differed in their regard of heresy.[15] For Perrone, when

[12] Femiano, S. D. (1967) *Infallibility of the Laity: The Legacy of Newman,* New York: Herder & Herder, p. 124.

[13] Femiano, S. D. *Infallibility of the Laity,* p. 124 (emphasis in original).

[14] *On Consulting the Faithful,* introduction by John Coulson, p. 23.

[15] Chadwick, O. (1957) *From Bossuet to Newman.* Cambridge: Cambridge University Press, pp. 182–184.

confronting heresy, the local bishops consult Rome and Rome declares the mind of the Church. For Newman, when confronting heresy, the mind of the Church has to be discovered by meditation, discussion and dialectic, including the faithful and hierarchy. Perrone's ecclesial structure is linear and hierarchical in the sense of a top-down, pyramidal model of leadership. Newman's is more inclusive rather than singular, and discursive rather than commanding.

SUMMARY OF THE ROLES OF LEADERS AND LAITY FROM *ON CONSULTING THE FAITHFUL*

The role that Newman envisages for laity again reflects a high view of lay people. First, they have a corporate responsibility to participate in the defining of doctrine. Theirs is not the only voice of discernment, and neither is it to determine alone, but their sense, general voice, belief and expressions of faith need to be taken into account. The source of their illative sense is the Holy Spirit enabling an individuative and collaborative contribution to the defining of doctrine. Second, lay people occupy a position of partnership with leaders in the witness of faith, and can rely on them to continue to define doctrine in the light of the fruit of that partnership. Third, lay people respond both in affirmation and *jealousy of error*. Although it is ultimately leaders that guard the faith, there are times when the laity will also exercise a remedial ministry.

On Consulting the Faithful argues that *consultation* means taking account of, reviewing and paying attention to the voice of the laity. This means that leaders need to listen, partly to hear an affirmation or rejection of what is proposed, and partly to learn something about themselves as if putting up a mirror. Both share in the task of the definition of belief and witness to the tradition. If adopted in this way, a theology of laity assumes a partnership role with a theology of ordination. One without the other is deficient. A theology of laity is crucial in the expression of both the direction and authority of the Church. Without it the Church becomes only notional. Yet, if a church is to become truly effective, direction and authority are only the foundations of its ministry. A true church must take mission seriously and in order to do this the *laos* will want to reflect on its faith. It will engage in what has popularly become known as doing theology. In fact the vitality of its missionary dynamic will depend on its confidence to do theology, and this in turn will depend on its equipping. Education in a more general sense will be considered later, but at this moment it is worth understanding the clergy-laity partnership in terms of theological reflection and mission.

WHO CAN DO THEOLOGY?

A fundamental assumption of *On Consulting the Faithful* is reflected in a contemporary question of who takes part in discovering theology, and this needs to be linked to Newman's educational project and ambition in order to gain a well-educated laity. Dennis Robinson suggests that a re-appropriation of Newman's epistomological categories will have consequences for the task of contemporary church education. Robinson elucidates it as follows. He first summarizes Newman's epistemological stance in four components:

> The first is the somewhat simplistic insight that truth is complex. The second is that the pursuit of truth is always imbued with a moral aspect, a place in a life of action. In other words knowledge is not passive; it has consequences. The third is that truth is a product not of individual and isolated reflection but of the life and vigour of the community. And the fourth is that truth, in its ultimate sense, is a particular Christian truth.[16]

His argument is in pursuit of a Christian university. He suggests that education within such a project will:

> provide an educational programme that is *necessarily* and *purposefully* broad and comprehensive. Second, education is an engagement of the whole person and is an active integration of the various and varying factors presented in the educational programme. Third, education is not a solitary pursuit, but takes place within the context of a community of learners and teachers. Finally, for Newman the only authentic university is a Christian university.[17]

If Robinson's argument is acceptable then what *On Consulting the Faithful* achieves is the following:

- lay people have an important role to engage in and contribute to the study and doing of theology
- theologians must expand their categories in order that lay people may be heard
- dialogue between academic and experiential theologians is crucial for a broader understanding
- dialogue should reflect a shared epistemological basis.

---

[16] Robinson, D. (2004), '*Sedes Sapientiae*: Newman, Truth and the Christian University' in *The Idea of a Christian University*, Astley, J. et al. (eds) Milton Keynes: Paternoster, pp 75–97 (p. 78).

[17] Ibid. p. 89 (emphasis in original).

Newman outlined his stance on a shared epistemological basis for education in the *Benedictine Essays,* namely that of a Benedictine monastic community. Today there are a number of approaches to doing theology, which reflect varying epistemological truth bases. In a new order of a theology of laity, no one size is likely to fit all. Newman's appeal for lay engagement in the theology of the Church clearly astounded some clergy of his day. Even though there has been little official attention given to it in church reports there are the beginnings of a movement to take seriously the contribution of congregations to do theology. What is needed is the will to pursue them.

Doing theology

There is not space, nor the remit here to outline the vast variety of approaches to doing theology,[18] especially by lay people. However, it is important to note that even though there has been little official attention paid to it, there is more interest in how congregations can contribute to the theological understanding of the Church as a whole. Martyn Percy, in *Engaging with Contemporary Culture,* outlines the way churches develop formative and transformative educational rationales.[19] He appeals for authentic engagement, by which he means that theology needs to be conversationalist. Using Lindbeck and Schreiter he advocates theology as public (congregations as well as specific individuals), practical (making links between belief and behaviour), plural (since congregations hold various theologies) and particular (articulating the self-conscious identity of the congregation). As has been seen, Hull delimits the field of who can do theology but he also argues for a distinction between theologizing and studying theology. He states: 'Theologising (which must be distinguished from the study of theology) ... takes place within the

---

[18] The point is made by Gavin D'Costa, in D'Costa, G. (2005) *Theology in the Public Square,* Oxford: Blackwell Publishing. He states that the history of theological education is complex and vast. Nevertheless, he provides a useful summary (pp. 5–20) echoing Edward Farley's larger treatment in Farley, E. (1994) *Theologia: The Fragmentation and Unity of Theological Education.* Philadelphia: Fortress Press. Also see O'Connell Killen, P. and de Beer, J. (1994) *The Art of Theological Reflection.* New York: Crossroad Publishing Company, pp. 46–110, and Kinast, R. L. (2000) *What Are They Saying About Theological Reflection?* New York: Paulist Press, pp. 6–63 for a taxonomy of approaches to theological studies.

[19] Percy, M., *Engaging with Contemporary Culture,* pp. 133–156.

community of faith, and its subject matter is the experience of the faithful, or of those who, knowing they are unfaithful, see even in this self-recognition a summons to faith'.[20] He concludes his argument with this statement: 'In other words, doing theology is characterized by participation in the intentionality of theologising, but studying theology is examination of the phenomenology of that intentionality and is thus characterized by empathy rather than by sympathy.' Those that Hull sees as participating in theologizing are of further interest to Astley who termed the phrase *Ordinary Theology*. He defines this as:

> Ordinary theology is my term for the theological beliefs and processes of believing that find expression in the God-talk of those believers who have received no scholarly theological education. Ordinary theology is routinely ignored by academic Christian theology. As John Hull put it at a symposium hosted by the North of England Institute of Christian Education in July 1996: 'If theology is what goes on in people's lives, we know amazingly little about Christian theology'.[21]

In a thorough treatment of his thesis, Astley makes the case for the study of *Ordinary Theology*, defending it from a variety of potential criticisms. He argues for a *liminal* church, one where Christians who exist on the threshold of the Church, enable, encourage and sometimes demand its doors to be opened. Ordinary theologians exist in open churches and often appear as anonymous Christians (Rahner) or in churches with open doors and great windows (Barth) or even the Church outside of the Church (Sölle). He concludes:

> Clearly these discussions raise profound questions for ecclesiology and the theology of Christian identity. In particular they bring us back to the question of the locus of authority or the beliefs of the Church. Most Churches distinguish different roles and offices within the Church, and locate authority differently ('appropriately') for different roles. But most will now allow the lay baptized *some* say in the debate about and definition of doctrine, if only by recognizing the importance of the exercise of reason in the pursuit of truth ... and of the 'primacy' or 'authority' of the conscience of the ordinary believer. A proper recognition of proper authority and hard-won freedom of belief are constituents of the practices that shape all Christian believers.[22]

Astley implicitly reminds us that what *OCF* was describing has not yet been fully realized. In the light of the insights of these authors, there is still some way still to go to appropriate a theology of laity which

---

[20] Francis, L. & Thatcher, A. (eds) (1990) *Christian Perspectives for Education*, Leominster: Gracewing, p. 5 (parentheses in original).

[21] Astley, J. *Ordinary Theology*, p. 1.

[22] Ibid. p. 162 (emphasis in original).

allows full engagement with, and contribution to the theology of the Church. However, the theology of the Church will not be complete without it, if for no other reason, as Astley states: 'Whatever we make of it theologically, speaking statistically ordinary theology *is* the theology of God's Church.'

LEARNERS AND MISSION

OCF assumes a relationship between clergy and laity by defining their distinctive roles. The collaboration, if it is to be ontologistically-based will provide an interrelationship of teaching and learning, interchangeable within the clergy and laity. True, it will often be the clergy who teach, but not always, and not particularly when it comes to reflecting on the wider context of society from a first-hand perspective. The exposing of faith and reason to this wider context generates opportunities to engage in mission in order to make plain what faith is, not only through continually seeking openings to influence polities, but also and rather more often, responding to those who are attracted to enquire. The processes are significant from a missiological perspective, for Newman advocates a method-ology of *presence*. To put it somewhat succinctly, the well-educated believer provides a presence in a situation, engages with others, and responds to what is heard and proposed. Zizioulas notes that a vicar in a church can only be genuinely vicarious when he or she is *present by participation*, not vicarious through absence. In a sense this is where the learner becomes the missioner and vice versa. The learner, and indeed missionary, has an obligation to engage with, and in a community. The learner is encouraged to enjoin with others and together they become a learning community participating in the processes, and enjoying the outcomes. In turn, the processes of learning outlined above also mark the presence of the learning community in the wider community, and the cycle continues. Newman is clear about the specific outcomes that pertain to the individual. He suggests that a person of faith benefits in this process by being encouraged towards maturity; *gaining ... proper confidence.* He is enabled in temperance; and *no longer ... dispirited or irritated.* He is also able to *fall back* upon self and find *calm* and *patience.*[23] As such, the life of faith becomes a cumulative cyclical journey of experiences, coping with and managing the development of body, mind and spirit.

---

[23] *Prepos.* pp. 390–391.

LEARNING AS A SACRAMENTAL PROCESS OF THE SPIRIT

Because Newman's educational methodology is constantly exposing what is internal to the individual or community, it could, in one sense be said to be sacramental. That which is within is made visible and offered to others, and this is with considerable consequence. For example, an apologetic is formed exposing, in his words, the *fictions and fallacies of opponents, explaining the charges against the Church,* and producing *independence of thought.*[24] In effect the sacramental process of learning challenges false views, brings enlightenment to the true nature of the Church and leads the believer towards a mature faith. It provides a crisis point of change, offering resolution and new confidence. It is often through crisis points that growth in faith takes place. Culler highlights this in his thesis, that Newman grew most in his faith journey through his illnesses.[25] In this way education begins to look like mission, asking and enquiring into the deeper questions of faith at life's crisis points.

Newman's connection between clergy, laity, education and mission and his insistence on coherence between them, suggests that the work of the Spirit is vital. It is the Spirit that teaches (1 Cor. 2.9-12), the Spirit that enables the presence of Christ in the world (Jn 14.15-21), and the Spirit that provides the witness within Christ's disciples (Acts 1.8). To undertake a project as vast as the contemporary church's mission imperative requires support from a well researched and understood pneumatology. Failure to do so will almost certainly contribute towards ecclesiological dysfunction. However, by exploring the metaphor of breathing together, Newman's *conspiratio,* the relationship between clergy and laity will begin to bear fruit. It will become part of the Church's mission as Christ is revealed, and it will order the Church so as to be inspired by the Spirit with Christ as its head.

MISSION AS EXPRESSED IN THE EPIPHANIC ROLE OF THE CHURCH

If mission is to be expressed through the Church's work, then it will need to be an instrument of revelation, something that the Church celebrates in the season of epiphany. This is highlighted by Rowan

---

[24] Ibid. pp 390–391.

[25] Culler, A. D. (1955) *The Imperial Intellect: A Study of Newman's Educational Ideal.* London: Oxford University Press, p. xii.

Williams, in *Anglican Identities*[26] when he focuses on key characters for Anglican formation from the Reformation to the latter part of the twentieth century. His twentieth-century choices are Michael Ramsey and J. A. T. Robinson. Ramsey was a key character in the ecclesial development of the twentieth century. Although Williams does not note Ramsey's connection with Newman, Owen Chadwick refers to it at various points in his biography,[27] suggesting that he was a disciple of Newman, loved reading his sermons and quoting him at times in the York diocesan letter. According to Ramsey's biographer, when visiting Rome he even discussed Newman with Pope Paul VI.[28] Williams links Ramsey to the Tractarians through Maurice whom he says was little read in Ramsey's day but provided a voice breaking through the Catholic and Protestant polemic. Most significantly, Chadwick concludes that Ramsey was an 'Anglo-Catholic leader and descendant of Newman and lover of Eastern Orthodoxy'. In particular he refers to Ramsey's love of Newman's sermons because of 'their awareness of the closeness of the divine behind the veil of matter'.[29]

According to Williams, Ramsey also formed links with Orthodox practice in biblical studies, Eucharistic theology and a theology of ministry.[30] He suggests a connection between Ramsey's *The Gospel and the Catholic Church* and Zizioulas' *Being in Communion,* which may be seen in the epiphanic role of the Church. Williams states 'the Church *is* the message ... it is first and foremost the epiphany of God's action, especially God's action in the paschal events'. This, according to Williams is Ramsey's sense of the epiphanic role of the Church. Zizioulas locates this role firmly in the Eucharistic community, laying out a theology of ordination that results in the ordained (within which he would count all the baptized) being inextricably linked with the community as ambassador and transformer. Williams, in his critique of Ramsey and Zizioulas pushes the role beyond the boundaries of the Eucharistic community. He extends the epiphanic role of the Church when he states: 'The Church may be perfectly the Church at the Eucharist, but its life is not exhausted in the Eucharist:

[26] Williams, R. *Anglican Identities,* pp. 87–120.

[27] Chadwick, O. (1991) *Michael Ramsey: A Life.* Oxford: Oxford University Press, pp. 34, 38, 96, 315, 321 and 335.

[28] Ibid. p. 321.

[29] Ibid. p. 96.

[30] Ibid. p. 96, which demonstrates a close parallel between Ramsey and Zizioulas.

there is a life that is always struggling to realize outside the "assembly" what the assembly shows forth'.[31]

Although Congar does not explicitly enter the discussion of the epiphanic role of the Church as outlined above, he concludes the second volume of his pneumatological work, *I Believe in the Holy Spirit*, with a section entitled *The Spirit Secretly Guides God's Work in the World*. In this, he links the fundamental activity of the Spirit in each generation relating the economies of the Father to the doxology of the Church. He states: 'The Church, who knows God and seeks his glory, wants to share that knowledge in order that God's glory may be increased'.[32] Congar sees lay people as having a primary role as living witnesses of Christ in their community. Zizioulas likewise affirms the ordination of the laity to participate in the epiphanic work of God, and Williams extends Zizioulas' epiphanic role to share the Christ of the Eucharist in the wider community. Within each of these views the relationship between Christ and the Spirit is vital.

THE RELATIONSHIP BETWEEN CHRISTOLOGY AND PNEUMATOLOGY FOR A THEOLOGY OF LAITY AND MISSION

It is clear that the relationship between pneumatology and Christology is important to any ecclesiology, and it is particularly significant for a theology of laity in the role of being and becoming the missioners of the Church. Within the pneumatology of both Congar and Zizioulas there are at least three pairs of concepts which relate laity, clergy and ecclesiology and strengthen the missionary imperative.

One and many

The first pair concerns the *one* and the *many*. Zizioulas maintains that the Holy Spirit, because of being *involved in*, but not *becoming* history as Christ did, enables the oneness of the Christ-event to become the experience of many and he relates this very visibly to the order of the Church's ministries. He states:

> The proper relationship between the 'one' and the 'many' must be maintained. In the case of the local Church the 'one' is represented through the ministry of the bishop, while the 'many' are represented through the other ministries and the laity. There is a fundamental principle in Orthodox ecclesiology going back to the early centuries and reflecting the proper synthesis between Christology and Pneumatology (sic) which I have been advocating here. This principle is

[31] Williams, R. *Anglican Identities,* p. 100.
[32] Congar, Y. *I Believe in the Holy Spirit,* Vol. II, p. 223.

that the 'one' – the bishop – cannot exist without the 'many' – the community – and the 'many' cannot exist without the 'one'.[33]

The significance of this is that without an emphasis on a theology of laity in a church, the activity of the Holy Spirit is diminished. The work of the Spirit is not recognized because the *many* are not recognized. Without a pneumatology, lay people (the *many*) are impotent, simply relying on an historical and exemplar Jesus of Nazareth, not one who is truly present in the event of the Church today and leading its mission.

Kenosis and exaltation

The second pair of concepts relates *kenosis* and *exaltation* derived from Congar's pneumatology. In attempting to formulate a pneumatological Christology, Congar suggests that Christology and soteriology should not be separated. He insists that 'the incarnation has an aim, and that aim is Easter, the resurrection and eschatological fulfilment'. His argument is that historical Christology has two states, the first of kenosis and the second of exaltation. Kenosis is revealed in Christ's obedience. Speaking of his quality as Son of God he states:

> What consciousness did he have, in his human soul, of his quality of Son of God? This is something that is hidden from us. The hypostatic union left his human soul, which was consubstantial with ours, in his human condition of *kenosis*, obedience and prayer.[34]

The second state is exaltation. Congar continues: 'The second decisive event leading to a new acquisition of Jesus' quality of son by virtue of an act of "God" through his Spirit is, of course, Jesus' resurrection and glorification'.

The importance of this pair for the mission of the Church is that just as Christ has two states, so too, the Church also has two states. As Christ was called to kenosis, so the Church is called to obedience to God and prayer for the world. It is also called to exaltation, to witness to the living presence of the risen Christ. The outcome of kenosis, for the ordained, is directed towards the Church's functions, and exaltation is the glorification of Christ within the Church. For the laity, the kenotic imperative is obedience to God and intercession for the world in a missionary capacity, and exaltation is a witnessing glorification of God.

---

[33] Zizioulas, J. D. *Being as Communion*, pp. 136–137 (emphasis in original).

[34] Congar, Y. *I Believe in the Holy Spirit*, Vol. III, pp. 166-167 (emphasis in original).

Without a high view of a theology of laity therefore, the Church will tend to emphasize kenosis and exaltation as they pertain to the ordained. Pneumatology will be limited to the boundaries of the Church and lacking that which is necessary for the glorification of Christ as a sign of hope for the world.

Institution and constitution

The third pair concerns institution and constitution. This brings pneumatology and Christology together in ecclesiology. Zizioulas explains that:

> If pneumatology is made constitutive of ecclesiology, the notion of *institution* itself will be deeply affected. In a christological (sic) perspective alone we can speak of the Church as *in-stituted* (by Christ), but in a pneumatological perspective we have to speak of it as *con-stituted* (by the Spirit).[35]

The prepositions *in* and *con*, when applied to the Church make a vast difference to mission and ecclesiology. The former represents the source and structure of the Church while the latter, the content and activity. Without them, the Church would suffer from a lack of origin and responsibility and ultimately not be able to exist. It needs foundations and formation, sources and development, framework and dynamic. Institution and constitution are both vital.

In terms of the mission of the Church, Christ's institution of the Church is remembered in the Eucharistic *anamnesis*. But Zizioulas adds a reminder: 'The *anamnesis* of Christ is realized not as a mere re-enactment of a past event but as an *anamnesis of the future*.[36]' This anamnesis re-members Christ in the community and re-members the community into Christ for the future work of ministry and mission. On this basis it is an eschatological work of fulfilment. It is a gift and a given, although this needs to be qualified, as Milbank suggests in *Being Reconciled:*

> The *methexis* of donation, which complements the *methexis* of language has two aspects. First of all, for theology there are no 'givens', only 'gifts'. Normally in our secular society, one can say, 'Oh there's a box', an inert 'given', and then maybe in addition one can say, 'yes, it was a gift'. But in Creation there are only givens in so far as they are also gifts: if one sees only objects, then one mis-apprehends and fails to recognize true natures. Here something can only be at all as a gift, and furthermore never ceases to be constantly given; in this case the act of giving is never something that reverts to the past tense.[37]

[35] Zizioulas, J. D. *Being as Communion*, p. 140 (emphasis and parentheses in original).

[36] Ibid. p. 254 (emphasis in original).

[37] Milbank, J. (2003) *Being Reconciled: Ontology and Pardon*. London: Routledge, p. xi (emphasis in original).

What was instituted by Christ, and perhaps appears to be a given, is actually and constantly constituted through the Spirit. Pneumatological Christology serves to deny ecclesiology from reverting to histori-cized institution. Within this, both clergy and laity are signs of the Kingdom, empowered to witness the founding work of Christ and the renewing work of the Spirit.

For clergy and laity to breathe together, both clergy and laity need to be distinctive, and well defined. A high view of the priesthood of the Church will ensure shape and purpose for the Church internally, as this is the primary role of the clergy. A high view of a theology of laity indicates an intention, whether conscious or not, to promote pneumatology, which in turn avoids some of the ecclesial diseases that beset the Church from time to time. As Zizioulas states:

> The fact that Orthodoxy has not experienced situations similar to those of Western Churches, such as the problem of clericalism, anti-institutionalism … may be taken as an indication that for the most part Pneumatology has saved the life of Orthodoxy up to now.[38]

It may have saved the life of Orthodoxy; the question now for other denominations is whether it will be allowed to perform its rescue operation once more. To do so, the voices and discernment of lay people must be heard and taken seriously as part of the vision of the Church.

QUESTIONS

- What can you learn from the ways in which clergy and laity work together in your church?
- What signs of pneumatology can you see expressed in the Church (or your church) today?
- How might it be possible to find out the 'Ordinary Theology' of a congregation?

---

[38] Zizioulas, J. D. *Being as Communion*, p. 140.

Chapter 8

NEWMAN'S THEOLOGY OF EDUCATION AND THE CHURCH AS A LEARNING COMMUNITY

All leaders need to take education seriously. In industry, training and retraining is essential to maximize the productivity of the workforce. In commerce, as new technologies grow and are introduced, continuous training is essential for the effective smooth running of companies. The Church, although not producing widgets, is providing a service, religious, social and theological to the community within and around it. Both leaders and members of the Church will need education to help them grow in faith, perform the ministry to which God has called and equipped them, and lead the people and ministries given them. Although this has been highlighted in the latter part of the twentieth century by concepts such as lifelong learning, it is not only a contemporary phenomenon.

Throughout the Christian era the education of church people has been an important factor in the growth of the Church. In the reformation of the Church after the seventh century Synod of Whitby, Bede tells of Bishop Cuthbert who set about teaching people of the new ways of being the Church.[1] Michael Papesh, in his book *Clerical Culture*, outlines the formation of clergy from the early Middle Ages during the rise of the Cathedral Schools.[2] Calvin's academy of Geneva trained people in the use of language. Through effective communication in writing and speaking, he demonstrated how to foster lay leadership.[3]

---

[1] Farmer, D. H. (ed.) (1965) *The Life of Cuthbert in The Age of Bede*, trans. by J. F. Webb. London: Penguin Books, pp. 41–104.

[2] Papesh, M. L. (2004) *Clerical Culture: Contradiction and Transformation.* Collegeville: Liturgical Press, pp. 61–76.

[3] George, T. (ed.) (1990) *John Calvin and the Church.* Louisville: Westminster/John Knox Press, p. 128.

Wesley set about his project with the support of classes for adults. So it is no surprise that Newman and the Tractarians found a way to educate clergy and lay people in the midst of the changes of the nineteenth century. It appears that every reformation needs education. If the present church is to change to meet the challenges of the new century then it needs to recognize the value of effective and strategic education, not simply for clergy, but also, and perhaps primarily, for laity.

It is important to note therefore that for a learning community to flourish there is a need to be truly holy in the sense of fully and deeply human. In order for this to be achieved a holistic education is vital. William Stringfellow said:

> Being holy does not mean being perfect but being whole. It does not mean being exceptionally religious ... it means being liberated from religiosity and pietism of any sort; it does not mean being morally better, it means being exemplary; it does not mean being godly, but rather, truly human.[4]

John Henry Newman's approach to education, which was formed a century before Stringfellow, endeavoured to be truly human.

NEWMAN'S EDUCATIONAL WORKS – A HOLISTIC EDUCATIONAL SCHEMA

Newman was quite definite about his primary ambition, a well-educated laity, and there is at least a hint at his disappointment concerning clerical education in the following:

> Seminaries are for the education of the clergy; Universities for the education of laymen. They are for separate purposes, and they act in separate spheres; yet, such is human infirmity, perhaps they ever will be rivals in their actual working. So at least it has been in time past.[5]

Although others in the Tractarian movement sought education for clergy, in *The Idea of a University* it is clear that Newman himself wishes to bring together a high view of laity and a robust theology of education. In the series of lectures known as the *Dublin Discourses*, which eventually became *The Idea*, he deals with both the curriculum and outcome for the student. The first discourses explore the purposes of a university, the branches of knowledge to be taught and the relationship of theology to other knowledge. In discourses

---

[4] Kellermann, B. W. (ed.) (1994) *A Keeper of the Word: Selected Writings of William Stringfellow.* Grand Rapids: Eerdmans, quoted by Bishop Peter Price (Bath & Wells) in his annual Archdeaconry Training Days, Sept. 2004.

[5] *Hist. III*, p. 240.

five to nine he examines a liberal process of education emphasizing knowledge for its own end, and the relationship of this to learning, professional skills and religion. He concludes with some comments on the duties of the Church with regard to knowledge. The style is precise, scrupulous and scholarly.

In contrast in another great work of education, *Rise and Progress of Universities,* Newman presents an imaginative view of his educational theology. In this work he uses metaphor, poetry and specific examples of historic characters to enable the reader to understand his principles. He reflects upon subjects such as the site of a university, Athens as a learning community, and historical contexts of learning from Rome through to Britain and Gaul. In doing this he builds a theology of education which is rooted in history, imagination and experience. As Tillman suggests, 'Newman was hoping imaginatively and constructively to render the university-idea real to the minds of his readers'.[6] She also makes a distinction:

> The argument drawn from Newman's historical imagination is not the comprehensive, theoretical and largely deductive argument of the 'Dublin Discourses'; rather, it is the complementary argument of concrete reasoning from antecedent probabilities and of retrospective reasoning from pattern instances.[7]

Although the style is different in the two works, the context is similar. Newman wrote his theology not only against the backdrop of growing liberalism, but also against the popularity of the Utilitarian project. It was inevitable then, remembering he was an occasional writer, that he would respond to the themes of liberal[8] and utilitarian education in the prevailing philosophy of his day. These are most under scrutiny in *The Idea,* and the work forms an apologetic for liberal education. However, in *Rise and Progress* he describes other educational landscapes – his beloved Oxford, the Catholic Church which had commissioned him to create a university, and his own relatively recent journey from Protestantism, which had resulted in the crisis which led him to conversion. Newman was a man who valued education in the university, the Church, and a person's own vocation. This left him passionate about lay people's understanding

---

[6] Newman, J. H. (1872–1873) [2001] *Rise and Progress of Universities and Benedictine Essays.* Leominster: Gracewing, p. xxxix.

[7] Ibid. p. xxxviii.

[8] Not to be confused with 'liberalism' to which he was opposed and which will be defined shortly.

of faith. Further, he was determined to provide opportunity to engage in education that would give courage to pursue the dictates of conscience.

The Idea was written as a series of lectures to support the university project which came about primarily because of a concern to provide education for Catholic laity.[9] However, the higher agenda of his enthusiasm was to defeat the growing liberalism prevalent in his time. The *Essay on the Development of Christian Doctrine* demonstrates what Newman meant by liberalism:

> That truth and falsehood in religion are but matter of opinion; that one doctrine is as good as another; that the Governor of the world does not intend that we should gain the truth; that there is no truth; that we are not more acceptable to God by believing this than by believing that; that no one is answerable for his opinions; that they are a matter of necessity or accident; that it is enough if we sincerely hold what we profess; that our merit lies in seeking, not in possessing; that it is a duty to follow what seems to us true, without a fear lest it should not be true; that it may be a gain to succeed, and can be no harm to fail; that we may take up and lay down opinions at pleasure; that belief belongs to the mere intellect, not to the heart also; that we may safely trust to ourselves in matters of Faith, and need no other guide – this is the principle of philosophies and heresies, which is very weakness.[10]

Dulles makes the point that Newman's course was to guide the believer, in a sense, through the *Scylla and Charybdis* of latitudinarianism and Evangelicalism with their respective reductionism and emotionalism. Dulles does not comment on how he achieved his balance, but he appears to do it by recourse to an analogy between dogmatism and confession, as Newman's own words suggest:

> Dogmatism was in teaching, what confession was in act. Each was the same strong principle of life in a different aspect, distinguishing the faith which was displayed in it from the world's philosophies on the one side, and the world's religions on the other.[11]

By examining dogmatism, and the guiding force behind it, he shows how a self-correcting conscience will educate the disciple:

> What Conscience is in the history of an individual mind, such was the dogmatic principle in the history of Christianity. Both in the one case and the other, there is the gradual formation of a directing power out of a principle. The natural voice of Conscience is far more imperative in testifying and enforcing

---

[9] Oxford University required students to sign up to The Thirty-nine Articles of Faith, a mainly Protestant text which meant that Catholics were effectively barred from some areas of higher education.

[10] *Dev.*, pp. 357–358.

[11] Ibid. p. 359.

a rule of duty, than successful in determining that duty in particular cases. It acts as a messenger from above, and says that there is a right and a wrong, and that the right must be followed; but it is variously, and therefore erroneously, trained in the instance of various persons. It mistakes error for truth; and yet we believe that on the whole, and even in those cases where it is ill-instructed, if its voice be diligently obeyed, it will gradually be cleared, simplified, and perfected, so that minds, starting differently will, if honest, in course of time converge to one and the same truth.[12]

This process of awareness of conscience to the fullness of missionary discipleship is best seen in the *Apologia pro Vita Sua* as he defends the processes of conscience and learning. The challenges of the final chapter say much about his ecclesiology and particularly his reinforcement of the parameters of the Church against the liberalism of the age. The authority of its infallibility and the discipline of its private judgment come into sharp contrast as he considers the dialectic of learning:

The energy of the human intellect 'does from opposition grow'; it thrives and is joyous, with a tough elastic strength, under the terrible blows of the divinely-fashioned weapon, and is never so much itself as when it has lately been overthrown. It is the custom with Protestant writers to consider that, whereas there are two great principles in action in the history of religion, Authority and Private Judgment, they have all the Private Judgment to themselves, and we have the full inheritance and the superincumbent oppression of Authority. But this is not so.[13]

In the heat of this dialectic, he explains the process further:

Catholic Christendom is no simple exhibition of religious absolutism, but presents a continuous picture of Authority and Private Judgment alternately advancing and retreating as the ebb and flow of the tide; it is a vast assemblage of human beings with wilful intellects and wild passions, brought together into one by the beauty and the Majesty of a Superhuman Power, into what may be called a large reformatory or training-school, not as if into a hospital or into a prison, not in order to be sent to bed, not to be buried alive, but (if I may change my metaphor) brought together as if into some moral factory, for the melting, refining, and moulding, by an incessant, noisy process, of the raw material of human nature, so excellent, so dangerous, so capable of divine purposes.[14]

In the journey from embryonic disciple to fully fledged missionary, there exists a process of gradually trusting conscience, accepting the teaching of dogmatism, forming confessional acts which results in a challenge to the prevalent philosophy. His subsequent missio-

---

[12] *Dev.*, p. 361.

[13] *Apol.*, (1865 edn.), p. 252 (emphasis in original).

[14] Ibid. (1865 edn.), p. 252 (parentheses in original).

logical methodology is a process of conscience building, learning, forming practical outcomes and finding confidence to defend action. Newman's assumption is that latent Christian principles of dogmatics already exist. They form guiding factors for discipleship for 'even before the Church had grown into the full measure of its doctrines, it was rooted in its principles'.[15] The overall outcome for the individual is to exert personal influence in the world and that this personal influence will be aligned to divine purposes. This is the foundation for Newman's theology of education and he depicts a view of laity which is well educated in liberal knowledge to combat the dangers of liberalism. The intended outcome is to utilize the instruments of the Church (Creeds, Eucharist, Scriptures, etc.) to become true disciples and missionaries.

WHAT MIGHT BE INCLUDED IN A CONTEMPORARY LEARNING CHURCH?

With the recent renaissance of adult education, lifelong learning, evening classes and late entry courses, the Church has to consider how it is providing learning opportunities for its adult membership. Each reformation in the Church has required education, so if the Church is to make the most of the opportunities of change before it at the moment, education, learning programmes and courses will become vital to success. On a more philosophical level, in a seminal book *What Prevents Christian Adults from Learning?* John M. Hull outlines the dangers and opportunities the Church might encounter if it is to become a truly learning community. His thesis is that without this the Church will become implausible both to the world and itself. It will simply lose its internal credibility and authenticity and become sectarian. He and an increasing number of educationalists who are concerned about faith have begun to form a phalanx of voices encouraging Christian leaders to take seriously their findings.

Hull's first examination in his book is of the Church in relation to modernity and he concludes that there are three possible reactions to it. Using Niebuhr's concepts of polytheism, henotheism (tribalism) and monotheism, and contrasting Christianity with Judaism, he describes the Christian Church as a church which embraces all people, but only in the religious aspect of their lives. What he means by this is that whereas Judaism embraces the totality of lives – a life style which incorporates all aspects of living – Christianity only

---

[15] *Dev.*, p. 361.

embraces a religious sensibility. He also attempts to suggest Judaism, while embracing the broader aspects of life only applies this to a small group of people, the Jews. Hence Christianity is prone to polytheism and Judaism to henotheism. His conclusion is that the Christian Church will be inclined to set up a henotheistic enclave that seeks to limit true loyalty to the faith by cutting off any outside critique.

But is Hull right to assert such a premise? Certainly in respect of parochialism where everyone belongs, or has a right to belong to the Church through being baptized into it, Christianity might be accused of a narrow influence on religious sensibilities. However, many other expressions of Christianity reject a territorial allegiance and would seek to attract believers who belong to a set of given doctrinal and behavioural norms. However, quite often in this second category, the premises behind the cultural norms are based purely on local inter-pretation and hence fall into Hull's trap of tribalistic (henotheistic) tendency.

Hull's point is that the educator has a responsibility of providing such an environment that people feel safe enough to move away from tribalistic behaviour and explore lands further away from home. This is not easy and quite often hindered by henotheistic drag such as isolation, a theology of leadership that places the local far ahead of any universal governance and a very strong liturgical identity. In other words, closed fellowships which exclude broader perspectives, with highly directive leadership, and often static in their worship traditions that bond the faithful together are hallmarks of a henotheistic expression of faith. Hull's concern is that in such an environment, people quit learning and hence never appropriate faith for themselves, remaining in a passive mode. His quest is to release the worshipper to find freedom to explore and forge faith for themselves, in communion with others. In order to do this he turns his attention to the way the ideology of faith is handled.

Hull discusses three forms of ideological stance, extra-ideological, inter-ideological and inner-ideological. In essence he is asking how self-critical a faith stance can be. His conclusion is that the educator must seek to provide experiences, resources and environments where the ideological aspect of faith can be examined from outside (extra-ideological), in relation to other faith perspectives (inter-ideological) and from within its own self-consistency (inner-ideological). He says:

> The discussion of ideology and religion has led us to define the task of the adult
> Christian educator as facilitating those kinds of learning experience which, not

delivering the Christian adult for ideology which would be both impossible and undesirable, do set him free from naïve and absolute ideological enclosure.[16]

Hull's thesis then, analyzes the various forms of faith development that were available to him when the book was written, including Fowler and Erikson's stages of faith development. His detailed analysis can be useful to practitioners. However, towards the end of the book he suggests that the classic doing–being dichotomy, that is, the polemic between a doing form of Christianity which is incarnational, here and now and visible, and the being form of Christianity, more mystical, beyond and invisible might perhaps not be the best form of dialectic. He advocates a state of *becoming* as more authentically Christian. Perhaps we perceive something here of the Augustinian option advocated earlier. Rather than trying to face the complexity of living in the world today by head-down activity, or fleeing into an ethereal embrace of the beyond, his mode is more eschatological. What is to be, is already here to be discovered, save that it is not yet. Becoming does not mean we have arrived, it means we are arriving at each moment of life in a new place. It does not mean that we are always on the move, for clearly each moment is a given place of rest, yet it is in the continuum of being transformed. It is the paradox of becoming that gives rise to learning, for to learn means to become aware of what meaning, value and opportunity for change is offered by experience. As a learning individual, this can be a life changing moment, a sudden or appreciable time of coming to terms with an experience of life. Occasionally this can happen seemingly spontaneously, but more usually there is at least some kind of educational regime that aids the learning – a school, mentor, or programme. For a learning community, such revelations of awareness can offer the same benefits as for an individual, but learning communities rarely *just happen*. They need some form of planning and nurturing.

Leadership for the Church, therefore, needs to understand at least some of the foundations of good adult education, its aims and purposes, if it is to form functional and practical ways of helping adults to learn. Malcolm Knowles suggests that for adults to learn best, the following will be true:

- They are free to direct themselves.
- They can connect their learning to their own knowledge and life experiences.

[16] Hull, J. M. (1985) *What Prevents Christian Adults from Learning.* London: SCM Press Ltd, p. 85.

- They are able to achieve their own goals.
- They can see the reason for learning something.
- What they learn is useful and practical.
- They are respected by their teachers.[17]

This is true for all adult learners, whether Christian or not, but for Christians there is also the possibility of developing a theology of education which may include the upholding of Christian values, endorsing the practical opportunities for ministry and providing opportunity for exploration of faith, as outlined by Hull above. This will be helpful if the Church is not to deny itself the rich benefits of learning and growth. If it does not, then Christian adults may be put off enriching and developing their faith. Hull outlines in his book some of the causes of the dysfunctional learning community, some of the reasons why Christian adults shirk responsibilities to learn. They include:

- It is not easy for some Christians to admit being baffled or even wrong.
- Like all adults – the fear of failure.
- Some results can be unwelcome – 'do theology and you'll lose your faith!' – 'do theology and you'll want to change things!'
- Adulthood is seen as the place which marks the end of learning.
- The world is so complex, Christians give up and retreat into a Christian world.
- Never having been taught how to learn.
- Everything is handed on a plate – dependency.
- Opportunities to learn are not offered or shared (no encouragement towards small groups or publicity about learning possibilities).
- Church language says, 'Don't bother' or does not reinforce learning or expectations are not taken seriously (the Church is not a conducive place to learn).

Clearly these are serious issues which church leaderships need to avoid or correct, and this may not be easy.

In the contemporary world of theology and education, Nicola Slee, in the final chapter of a compendium of essays on theology and adult education, *Adult Education and Theological Interpretations* reflects

---

[17] Adapted from the summary of Knowles' andragogy (a term for adult education that Knowles introduced) at www.infed.org/thinkers/et-knowl.htm.

on the contributions of the essayists. Under the title *Endeavours in a Theology of Adult Education*[18] she makes a number of salient points for such a theology. First she recognizes that all academic endeavour is hermeneutically committed.[19] The authors of theologies of education will be shaped by personal life experience and the wider cultural, social and political context. Second, she outlines the reasons why not many people attempt developing a theology of adult education. This includes the lack of an institutional context, the secularization of education, the lack of vision from churches, and the impact of patriarchal undervaluing of education. She suggests that the task is complex as the two disciplines are specialized and require a thorough grounding and competence in both.

She outlines three potential tensions of a theology of education – individual versus communal, cognitive versus affective and developmental versus conversion perspectives. These, she says:

> are themselves symptomatic of a more basic tension between various competing philosophical and theological traditions upon which different authors draw for their reflections. On the one hand the emphasis on education as an essentially cognitive and developmental process of individual meaning-making has its roots in the traditions of Enlightenment rationality, Existential philosophy, and Protestant liberalism … On the other hand, the emphasis on education as an activity of the whole person in community through the activities of creative imagination, vision and contemplation leading to political action, arises out of very different philosophical traditions, namely those of Marxist socialism, postmodernism and feminism and related forms of liberation and feminist theologies.[20]

Finally she offers some resources for constructing a theology of education:[21]

- Biblical – the use of wisdom, prophetic, and Gospel traditions, corresponding to knowledge-based, socially conscious and Christological perspectives.
- Creational – recognizing that a creation centred spirituality, replacing anthropocentric redemption/fall paradigms, is more in keeping with the contemporary ecological crisis.
- Contemporary – theology that is concerned to recapture a more holistic understanding of personhood, determining theological anthropology.

[18] Nicola Slee in Jarvis, P. and Walters, N. (eds) (1993) *Adult Education and Theological Interpretations*, Malabar: Krieger Publishing, pp. 323–346.

[19] Ibid. p. 325.

[20] Ibid. pp. 334–335.

[21] Ibid. pp. 337–345.

- Soteriology and Christology – giving rise to notions of education being salvific and redemptory, promoting fulfilment in and development of the individual.
- Ecclesial and communal – the learning community and church sharing mutual tensions, at the margins of society, functioning within it and reflecting its values, pointing to something beyond, living within the tension of the domestic and missionary, living within a utopian ideal as well as a daily fragility.

These ecclesiological and eschatological insights are a useful reminder of the parameters of any theology of education. It would be anachronistic to expect Newman adequately to fulfil any of the above categories in contemporary theological understanding; however it would be equally neglectful not to note how the theology of adult education, present in *The Idea* in fact does correspond with much of what Slee suggests.

For example, Newman's university project promoted a utopian ideal in its liberal foundation and methodology and because of the utilitarian project, found itself in need of vigorous defence. The promotion of fulfilment and development of the individual is written large over many of the discourses. These ambitions afford his educational thinking a high and Christian anthropology derived from soteriological and Christological perspectives. But further, what Newman provides is an educational theory that is based on enlargement, discipline and habit, promoting holistic outcomes rather than functional, consumerist or mechanistic ones. He adopts a liberal technique very different from that which is defined in some parts of the contemporary church as liberal education.[22] His kind of liberal education enables a person to find meaning and process to deal with experience. It is akin to a truly genuine praxis.

Newman locates educative enquiry between conscience and church, by which he means between the individual sense of conscience and the infallibility of the Church. He toasts the Pope, but also conscience. In one sense, and clearly a limited sense, this is where

---

[22] Compare, for example, Craig's model of liberal education in Craig, Y. (1996) *Tomorrow is Another Country*, GS misc. 467, London: Church House Press, pp. 36–37, where liberal education is defined as a commodity to fill the learner, very much like the 'banking' education that Paulo Freire deplores in the second chapter of Freire, P. (1972) *Pedagogy of the Oppressed*, trans. by Myra Bergman Ramos, Harmondsworth: Penguin Books. The learner is mistakenly seen as a receptacle only able to contain educational facts.

churches need to position themselves – Catholic and reformed, part of the universal, yet cognisant of the individual. They may have great difficulty in reconciling these positions, but an educative process can exploit them. A liberal process of education, as outlined by Newman could be a useful instrument to achieve this. It is a process that enables lay people to explore faith in the wider historical and ecclesiastical context.

What might this look like in a church context?

No one shape will fit all in the provision of a liberal process of education for clergy and laity. However, some guiding principles might be to offer a safe place to learn, where learning is deemed not only useful, but also enriching. Leaders, like everyone else will show that they too want and need to learn because by their example others are more likely to believe it to be a worthwhile activity. Access to learning is crucial and thoughtful research as to when, where and how learning opportunities are offered will contribute to the success of learning schemas and events. Good programme designs will enable good learning. They are usually based on a single aim, relevant objectives, appropriate methodologies, a high standard of implementation, and effectively evaluated both immediately and in the medium and long term. This will alleviate some of the adult education principles highlighted above, but they do not appear overnight. However, it is possible to evaluate church activities for their potential to teach and help the congregation to learn. In one parish I served in a need to help some of the frail elderly with simple household tasks, cutting down bushes, mending doorbells and the like became a learning exercise (and in fact eventually an exercise in mission too). The leadership team had noted that there wasn't much opportunity for men to get together in the Church. A deliberate, yet somewhat *un-PC* decision was made to ask some men to get together to help. A group began and the informal learning that took place, about skills, social issues and faith was enormous. Another time, a mixed group of business people formed themselves into a seminar group to share problems and challenges at work. The group not only shared practicalities, but also began to reflect theologically on issues that emerged from their discussion.

Learning communities, like all communities take a time to bond, a time to establish and careful support to sustain them, but if the Church is going to grow it is essential that leaders pay attention to learning. If the Church is truly to find a place in society, to exert personal influence, it must learn how to speak to the issues that surround it with the kind of liberal knowledge Newman advocated. If it wishes to announce the good news to the generations it serves or re-announce the Gospel to those who have all but forgotten it, it must rediscover the ability to learn and enlarge its reflection. If Newman is right then this will enable it to express faith through personal influence. Contemporary educationalists offer method and resource for this task in order that both clergy and lay people can discover the joy of learning.

QUESTIONS

- Do you agree with Hull's analysis of what prevents adult Christians from learning? How would you like to add to it or change it?
- In what way is it possible to interpret Newman's understanding of education in today's world?
- What signs are there that the Church (or your local church) is a learning community?

Chapter 9

GOD, MINISTRY AND TIME

One of the major preoccupations of people living in the industri-
alized world is time. It has been said that in the UK we work longer
hours than any other nation in the European community. Often the
higher up a person works in a company, the longer the hours seem
to be, especially when very high salaries are being paid to senior
executives, often at the cost of a loss of personal time. Many of these
are commuters with long or time consuming journeys to get to work.
Time management courses abound for managers to enable them
to maximize what can be achieved in a day or a week. On the other
hand, the leisure industry constantly reminds us of where we can
spend time to recuperate from the stresses and strains of modern
living by getting away from it all.

Those who occupy leadership positions in the Church are not
exempt from these pressures either. The nature of the role often
means that they feel that there is no point at which the job has been
done and no time when they are off duty so that any diminution of
total availability can be seen as some kind of failure with detrimental
effects on their family, friendships and personal health. Very often this
can be accompanied by a sense of being driven. Preaching salvation
by grace or faith, the driven leader actually practises salvation by
works. He or she must be perfect, must be strong with an obligation to
make everyone happy and to meet all their needs. Such leaders pack
their days so full that they are late for every meeting or appointment
as they struggle to balance every plate, juggle all the balls, frenetically
baling out the water while holding onto both sail and rudder, fearing
that the barque of Christ will sink beneath the waves.

This is the description of the workaholic or the do-it-all leaders.
Much of this behaviour is really a defence against an increasing fear

of helplessness and failure coupled with an acute anxiety about ever letting go or of delegating. Unclear about their role, they are unable to know the difference between what is important and what is urgent or have any real strategic or prioritizing skills, some leaders simply sink into frozen immobility like a rabbit caught in a car's headlights or pursue all sorts of activities which are really a form of avoidance or procrastination.

Thinking about time raises psychological questions – why is it, I can never say no? – as well as a realization of the need to learn certain skills and techniques. However, for the Christian, it is important to stress that it is a spiritual issue as well. How should we regard time in the light of Revelation?

The author of the Letter to the Ephesians urges the Christian to:

> Be careful then how you live, not as unwise people but as wise making the most of the time, because the days are evil. So do not be foolish, but understand what the will of the Lord is.[1]

Michel Quoist comments on this text:

> And so all men run after time, Lord.
> They pass through life running-hurried, jostled, overburdened,
> Frantic, and they never get there. They haven't time.
> In spite of all their efforts they're still short of time,
> Of a great deal of time,
> Lord, you must have made a mistake in your calculations,
> There's a mistake somewhere,
> The hours are too short,
> The days are too short,
> Our lives are too short.
> You who are beyond time, Lord, you smile to see us fighting it,
> And you know what you are doing,
> You make no mistakes in your distribution of time to men.
> You give each one time to do what you want him to do.[2]

The Bible speaks of two kinds of time: cosmic time over which the cycles of nature rule and historical time which unfolds itself in the course of actual events. God governs them both and will bring them together towards the same goal and fulfilment. In Genesis 1.5 God the Creator has established the rhythms which nature obeys, the alteration of days and night, the movement of the stars, the changes of the seasons with which humanity is called to be in harmony. All religions,

[1] Ephesians 5.15-17.
[2] Quoist, Michel (1963) (English translation) Anne Marie de Commaile and Agnes Mitchell Forsyth, *Prayers of Life.* London: Gill and Macmillan, p. 77.

including Judaism recognized a sacred significance in this which religious festivals and practices celebrated. God in his Revelation has, however, made these memorials also of the great acts of God in history, so that the consecration of time, with which the Jewish people were so familiar, made the entire existence of humankind enclosed in a network of rites and celebrations which sanctified it.[3] It is this insight that is enshrined in the Christian liturgy also. Living in a cyclical manner, based on celebration, remembrance and a fundamental rhythm is essential both to being human but also to remind us that all things will return to the God who is the author of all time.

In history we have a complementary understanding of time being orientated by the design of God which is gradually unveiled and manifested in it. It is characterized by unique events which are not repeated. There is a sense of moving forward, of progress, of salvation history in which God enters time to shape human affairs towards the end time and judgment. The experience will be one of both darkness and light and struggle within a sinful world with a promise of a new age of justice and happiness.[4] Jesus reminds us that the time of God's intervention in history is reaching fulfilment when he unrolled the scroll of Isaiah in the synagogue and also declared that the kingdom of God has come near.[5] Christians thus are called to live with a sense not only of cosmic and of historical time but also of this being a special time in which they are called to make this real in their own lives by living out their vocation.

John Henry Newman (1801–1890) in his *Meditations and Devotions*, intended for use by his parishioners in Birmingham, gives this a perspective in the context of creation and vocation. He writes:

> God was all-complete, all blessed in Himself; but it was His will to create a world for His glory. He is Almighty and might have done all things Himself, but it has been His will to bring about His purposes by the beings He has created. We are all created to His glory – we are created to do something or to be something for which no one else is created; I have a place in God's counsels, in God's world, which no one else has; whether I be rich or poor, despised or esteemed by man, God knows me and calls me by my name.[6]

This all-sufficient God chose to need the human race to accomplish his purposes for humankind so that it is our calling first of all to

---

[3] Exodus 12.23; 23.16; Lev. 23.10; 2 Kings 16.15 and many other texts.
[4] Hosea 2.20ff; Is 11.1-9.
[5] Luke 4.17-21; Mk 1.15.
[6] Newman, J. H. (1893), *Meditations and Devotions* (2nd edn) London: Longmans, p. 400.

respond to the vocational roll call and be in some sense co-creators with God who is the source of our being and also Christ's hands and feet in the time that has been given to us. He continues:

> God has created me to do Him some definite service; He has committed some work to me which He has not committed to another. I have my mission – I may never know it in this life, but I shall be told it in the next. Somehow I am necessary for His purposes, as necessary in my place as an Archangel in his – if indeed, I fail, He can raise another, as he would make the stone the children of Abraham. Yet I have a part in this great work; I am a link in a chain, a bond of connexion between persons. He has not created me for naught. I shall do good, I shall do His work; I shall be an angel of peace, a preacher of truth in my own place, while not intending it, if I do but keep His commandments and serve Him in my calling.[7]

Newman is talking here not just about the vocation of all the baptized but of all humans who need to have a realization that by God's grace, each of them has a mission, a calling, and a part in God's work. One aspect of mission must therefore be to awaken this sense in everyone, enabling them to realize that they can fulfil this calling wherever they are. It is an anthropological statement also for it is of the nature of what it means to be human to be an instrument of God and a partner with him. This is what time is for and it is for a greater realization of this that we should pray:

> Deign to fulfil Thy high purposes in me whatever they may be – work in and through me. I am born to serve thee, to be Thine, to be Thy instrument.[8]

This understanding of the time that we have been given by God offers a very different way of thinking about human life, the world and the work we do than the rather utilitarian model that seems to be increasingly prevalent in a secular society. God is still creating, sustaining and saving the world, but through and with us as Christ's disciples. What we have to do is to try and discern how we can do that and distance ourselves from any activities which are destructive of God's creativity, saving power and care for the world we live in. A purely economic sense of time which measures success or failure in terms of productivity runs the risk of seeing human life as disposable when economic usefulness is over, so that all forms of human endeavour are but exploitation for personal gain. Knowing that we are needed by God can be uplifting to the human heart, even when we may be burdened by illness or adversity, so that it can be through suffering

---

[7] Ibid.
[8] Ibid. p. 401.

that something of God's purpose in working through us is being accomplished. Living by the rhythm of cosmic time helps to prepare the mind and heart for the ministry that all are called to do within historical time.

A Christian view of time sees it therefore as a gift to be used well and with an awareness of why it has been given. It is not just for our benefit so that we, as individuals, may find God, but for the benefit of others also. Time is the great leveller for we are all part of it. It is something to which we are subject and which we share. A sense of this is an awareness of vocation and requires the right disposition (habitus) within us.

Time is not only a gift, but also a gift that requires a skill; for using time as God wants us to use it, has to be learnt and practised. What it should be used for at any moment requires the development of discernment and wisdom.

Since time is a gift from God, we need to regard it not so much as a possession over which we have sole rights but as something entrusted. We are *stewards of time* just as we are also *stewards of creation*. The fact that God not only created time but entered it and lived it means that we can look to Jesus Christ as a model for the use of time. Some of the things that he did were regarded by his disciples as a waste of time.

We therefore need a Christological sense of time which has an eschatological dimension; we have both to be ready for what is coming because we are in an in-between time but also we have to be engaged with the ordinary things of life and to do these well. The Liturgical Year provides an important icon of time in which eternity and history become intermingled, but which also portrays a seasonal cycle of death, birth, renewal and growth. This was important when considering leadership in change.

If we examine how the word *time* is used in our language we can see that it is a word very like *money*. We talk of spending time, wasting time, being short of time, time well spent, saving time, giving time exactly as we do when speaking about money.

However, as with money, we need to know whose time it is. Does it belong to us or to someone else? Is it time we can use as we like or is it time that has been entrusted to us to spend on behalf of the organization to which we belong? These are highly relevant issues when at work and in many other contexts.

Further questions can be asked about time. Whose time is it? Is this our own time or have we to spend the time as directed by others or as the job demands with some areas of discretion? An employee during working time is being paid for his/her time and therefore certain obligations follow.

Pressing this analogy further, we can realize that just as we can receive money from someone else or give it to them, so we can be given time by another person or we can give time to them, provided that it is ours to give.

Seen like this, time is like a transaction or a contract. A long-term disposal of time between two people might better be described as a *Covenant* in which there is an agreement about how it is to be used or spent. Rather like the Exodus, time is spent to undertake some kind of journey or project which may have implications for how the participants live and the values that they have.

A critical question to be asked with time as with money as in all human areas of activity, is where is the ownership? Only then can we resolve the question of what we may do with the time that we have at any moment. What we need to notice is that if time is like money and we give a promise of time to someone else, there is a change of ownership as there is when we agree to work for someone or when we receive a gift or loan of money. Thus the person who gives it no longer has the same freedom as they had before and this may apply to the recipient also.

Time in this sense can be categorized as follows:

- **Personal** time to do with what we want i.e. wholly at our disposal.
- **Delegated professional** time which we may use largely as we think fit to do the job which we have been given i.e. we have delegated authority to use it according to our professional judgment to fulfil the role that we have, but within parameters and guidelines that go with that.
- **Specified professional** time which has been allocated by others for a specific purpose and which is therefore non-negotiable.
- **God's** time when we attend to our relationship with God. This may be a subdivision of personal time or part of my professional time or a combination of both or something that is seen separately. In an important sense, however, *all* time is God's time to be used and enjoyed in His name.

If time is rather like money and may be gifted (and tithed) then there is a change of ownership which has implications for how we behave.

If we give time to another, it is no longer our time whether personal or professional, just as if we give a person money, it is no longer ours. Therefore we have to honour that gift. If we do not and allow that time to be taken up by others, then is this not rather like theft?

On the other hand, if we receive the gift of another person's time, then we have ownership of it in some sense. It is an abuse of our rights if it is arbitrarily taken away similar to someone coming back having given us money and demanding it back or cancelling the cheque!

This raises a number of issues, not least about claims made on our time and also interruptions. If we are not careful we may be adopting a style of leadership which involves a good deal of time stealing and giving of short change!

The aim is to be *responsive* rather than *reactive*. To be responsive means adopting methods for the giving of time which are thought through and prioritized so that promises are not made which cannot be kept. Proper attention is given to the recipients so that they feel listened and attended to. Interruptions are kept to an absolute minimum or properly managed to that there is no time-stealing. Organizations that are well known for this have a high degree of customer satisfaction and are much less likely to be plagued by destructive conflict. Time is not wasted because it is properly targeted.

Leaders who seek to be responsive have to learn to say no as well as yes but in ways which convey a sense that the person asking for time will be attended to appropriately and when that happens it will be worthwhile. This requires the adoption of assertive rather than submissive or aggressive behaviour. Using time in this way is very motivating once the employee or the Church members get used to thought through strategies for responding to requests for the leader's time. The wide range of technological aids available have made the management of interruptions much easier but should be used thoughtfully. Emails need to be answered or at least acknowledged within a reasonable space and recorded phone messages followed up, which means time set aside to do this. Recorded or standard messages that reside on answering machines or the out-of-office facility need some thought also for they convey as much by how they say what they do as they do by the content.

Responsive strategies lead to:

- The giving of high quality time which maximizes effectiveness.
- A strategic use of time by the leadership.
- A sense in the organization of being properly attended to even if this means a little delay.

- Increased motivation from volunteers and employees.
- More assertive behaviour with better outcomes.

Reactive leadership behaves exactly like a billiard ball which moves around the table having been entirely pushed by others. Whoever was the last person to badger me gets our time and interruptions are not managed so that time that has been given to one person is *stolen* by others. Promises of time will frequently be broken or not properly fulfilled. This is a major source of conflict in an organization. Organizations which are reactive in this way have little sense of priorities and sacrifice giving high quality attention to trying to please everyone by saying yes, even when they cannot deliver what has been promised. Behaviour will typically be both submissive and aggressive; submissive in that it leaders are driven by a desire to please, to be liked, or to appear to be able to jump over buildings. They sometimes therefore become aggressive when the stress becomes too much and the demands too great but more often go into avoidance mode. Such behaviour causes an enormous amount of conflict which then turns to apathy, de-motivation and a loss of faith in the leadership. The danger of the *Lone Ranger* or *Do-it-all style* of leadership is that it cannot deliver all that is required in the time and so must fail.

Reactive ways of working therefore lead to:

- Little high quality time being given.
- A loss of any strategic sense of leadership or management.
- Confusion between what is important and what is immediate.
- A sense in the organization that it is unlikely that one will ever be properly attended to.
- Markedly decreased motivation.
- Usually submissive behaviour which may flip into aggressive behaviour.
- High levels of conflict or a considerable apathy.

Managing time well therefore is not only essential for a healthy organization, especially a church, but also for the good health of those who are its leaders. The proper balance between personal time and professional time then becomes an important spiritual model for church members in how to live as Christians with a sense of God's calling and of living in God's time.

Many writers suggest that being perfect means no more than 'performing the ordinary duties of the day well' and as Quoist suggests that God has given us sufficient time to do what he wishes us to do,[9] then it is clearly important that the Christian vocation is seen as something which uses time as a resource which is God-given.

It is not about increasing the *oughteries* or the feelings of guilt but of seeing time like creation itself as an entrusted gift to be used well, worked with but also to be enjoyed and celebrated.

This approach to time is not intended to negate the many valuable books and training aids which are available to help busy people use time more effectively. Most of these are designed to help people use time more efficiently to benefit the organization economically. Time wasted is costly in financial terms, for time is money or so we think. Often in our society what is worth doing is measured in this way and valued or not, in terms of its cost effectiveness. In a very utilitarian world, many uses of time may therefore be in danger of being under-valued; the nurse spending time talking with the elderly patient, the priest turning up at the coffee morning, the head teacher *loitering* and talking with the pupils during the break or at lunchtime or the manager spending time at the cash till talking with those who staff the check-outs, the mother or father who give up their career for a time to be with their young child, the impecunious artist, the poet, the monk who prays in his cell, the cathedral choir at evensong, have a value which is not measurable in quantitative terms. What may be a waste of time to many may actually be what really enriches us.

Of course, mastery of certain basic techniques such as working with a tidy desk, a proper filing system, prioritizing tasks, proper management of meetings, appointments and interruptions through effective diary control, having SMART goals and so forth have their place in the life of a church leader as a means to an end, which is to give time to others in the furtherance of God's purposes, of which one will be spending time with the people whom the world has no time for and on things which it may despise or regard as useless. It is also often true that mismanagement of the techniques of efficient time management may inhibit the carrying out of just those activities which are *useless* in the world's eyes.

One classic example of this is the way in which clergy often mismanage appointments through being reactive rather than responsive. To allow constant interruptions when spending time with a distressed parishioner is to allow his time to be stolen, for though it is the clergyperson's professional time, it has been given and covenanted to someone else and should not be arbitrarily taken away.

[9] Ibid. p. 381.

Interruptions cannot be eliminated totally but they can be managed and modern technology is there to be used. Nothing detracts from a church leader's effectiveness more than an inability to give high quality time to others, for time more than money or goods, is what the Church can and should give freely. Listening to the stories of others may well be the most important skill that should be developed in church leaders and finding time for that a very high priority.

Another area that requires careful attention and the dedication of time is delegation. The Church is largely made up of volunteers who give of their time freely but that does not mean that care should not be taken to ensure that they know what they are doing, to support and monitor what they do and show appreciation when they have done it. The time issue here can best be expressed by a series of questions which the would-be volunteer needs to have answered. They often don't ask these but at some stage will wish they had! It will be time well spent by the leadership for it is a kind of contract.

THE MORAL CONTRACT FOR VOLUNTEERS

- What do I/we need to know about this role?
- What exactly do you want me to do?
- When do you want me to do it?
- How much time will it involve?
- Who will I do it with?
- Where?
- What Health and Safety matters do I need to be aware of?
- Will I need CRB clearance and if so, who will arrange it?
- For how long do you want me to do it?
- What decisions will I be expected to make and what must I refer to others?
- Will others who need to be told, be made clearly aware of what I am to do?
- What are the different roles in the Church and how does what you want me to do fit in with these?
- Could you spell out clearly what my responsibilities will be?
- What are my rights under legislation and the policy of the Church?
- Who will I be answerable to?
- How will I be supported?
- Will there be opportunities for ongoing training to develop my capacity to do this?
- Will my necessary expenses be repaid to me?

- When will I be inducted into the role and by whom?
- May I make suggestions?
- What else don't I know that I need to know?
- Am I really the right person for this?
- If I have problems, who do I go to and how will they be handled?
- What are your expectations of me?

Attention to these matters may save a great deal of time and conflict or misunderstanding later. When things go wrong in churches, the hurt is usually greater because there is an expectation that a higher standard of care will be exercised than in other organizations. On the occasions when this does not happen, there is a natural feeling of betrayal, which may result in a loss of credibility for all that the Church says it stands for. Recent history in Ireland, for example, has illustrated this very well. There are a number of different reasons why people volunteer – the need to be needed, the desire to be part of a community of interest, the desire to make a difference – but attention to the above which means that they will be properly handled is also important. Delegation is not abdication but often ends up that way.

PRIORITIZING TIME – AN ECCLESIOLOGICAL QUESTION

What a leader should predominantly spend his or her time on will depend on a number of factors. There are a number of generic tasks that need to be carried out but a leader must also make an assessment of the needs of the congregation(s), their history and what skills and talents are available among the laity and fellow clergy. A wise leader becoming an incumbent, parish priest or new minister will spend time in making some kind of audit of where people are spiritually, their needs, and their openness to change and what obstacles may need to be overcome if things are to move forward. Some priorities may be determined by what is called churchmanship and what overall view of the nature of church and the ordained role is predominant. However, if leadership is to be at all strategic, then time has to be allocated for the processes necessary to lead effectively in change. Leaders need to ask themselves where their presence may be strategically important. The *tambourine* model of church (discussed in Chapter 4) comes into its own here because it allows church leaders to spend their time where it is most needed and not be *imprisoned* by the stereotypical *pyramid* model.

Dulles' models of the Church are helpful here since the adoption of any one or more of the images to characterize what is felt to be important at any one time, has implications for prioritizing of time, resources and energy.

Clearly, there needs to be an institutional element in any church organization. Procedures have to be devised and followed and management must be competently done, for a failure to do this may lead not only to legal consequences but also to frustration at inefficiency and incompetence about the carrying out of even basic tasks. A feeling of injustice is often experienced in badly run organizations. Often the larger the church, the more bureaucracy there is, but it does not have to be like this. Unfortunately, institutionalism can become an end in itself absorbing more and more energy as people increasingly have to resource maintenance rather than mission. Arguably, the Church was a movement before it became an institution and needs perhaps to remind itself of the importance of travelling light. Many of the abuses of the past in the history of the Church have been due to institutionalism of one kind or another with all the problems of power that goes with it. The importance of jurisdiction and visible unity as well as well-thought out bureaucratic procedures will be important.

The biblical images that Dulles identifies all have potential to energize and give a sense of direction to a Christian community. They also have implications for what priorities the leadership should have. For example, the image of *Mystical Body* will emphasize the importance of the spiritual, of worship as mystery. To make this real, the Church will need to develop opportunities for spiritual guidance, reflection and prayer, to stress liturgical symbolism, solemnity and ritual and to reflect this also in teaching about the divine nature of the Church and its indwelling by the Spirit. The building as a place of prayer with suitable visual symbols to aid that understanding will be important. The formation of the laity in the liturgy and their appropriate place within it would be very high priority also.

By contrast the image of the Church as the *People of God* is likely to be much more informal. Stress here will be on the provisionality of the Church and the importance of journeying. It is likely that structures will be much more flexible and open to change and therefore a more pragmatic approach to leadership may be appropriate. Because there is an element of risk in this image, there would be a stress on being an adult Christian but one who is not too wedded to structures. A different kind of leadership would be expected here than in the previous model. Motivational skills will be vital for the leadership and a willingness to be mobile among the different spheres of the *tambourine*.

In the *Church as Sacrament,* there would be a strong Eucharistic emphasis and community sense. Hence the leadership would spend quite a lot of time on community formation and resourcing. Since here liturgy as celebration is so important, much might be made of opportunities for the Eucharist to express this and to draw different groups in. A welcoming ethos will be emphasized and modelled here. Active participation will be important as will be the sense of people going out as leaven in the world, making Christianity known by the living of it. Some teaching will need to back this up. Much preparation will go into the making of liturgy and this will require some orchestration. Flexibility in worship will be key here and a sense of what may be appropriate boundaries. This will be quite a permissive culture.

The *Church as Herald* model's emphasis on proclamation and conversion will indicate where a lot of time will need to be put into teaching the laity and on means of making the Gospel known. Hence communication will be a top priority here as well as a visible presence of the Church in public places and where its influence can be felt. Getting the message across through the media and in other ways will occupy much of the leadership's time. Less time will be spent on symbolic ways of communicating as this is very much a model of making the Word known. Hence a strong, authoritative emphasis in teaching and instruction would be expected from the leadership.

On the other hand, the *Church as Servant* places much more emphasis on dialogue and service to the world. It is concerned to work alongside other agencies or people who have similar social aims. The leadership here would need to be a very community minded group of people who can reassure the congregation of the importance of the option for the poor but also be able to communicate a sense of welcome to all without preconditions. A welcoming, open door ethos would need to be built up as well as good links with secular agencies. Time would need to be spent forging these outside the *tambourine* altogether.

The *Church as Disciple* has a similar features to the *Herald* in that it stresses the countercultural nature of Christianity to some extent and the need to risk all for Christ but is less hierarchical, more open to the idea of all being learners together. Teaching is likely to be more open-ended and there would be a strong emphasis on adult education as distinct from instruction. It will have a collaborative educational approach in which the leadership participates. Time would need to be spent encouraging the right kind of ethos for this and the resources to underpin it. Collaborative ways of working become particularly important in this model as does the setting up of teams that reflect on and learn from their work together.

None of these images are mutually exclusive, but it is likely that a church might wish to major on some of them. This can be done in two ways; either to adopt some of them for a time as an emphasis for a particular phase of its growth and development, or more permanently, as expressing a longer-term commitment. In both cases, the implications for the use of time, resources and energy will need to be worked through as part of the strategy for change. What must be avoided are vague declarations of intent which never get translated into practice because the leadership does not appreciate the implications of what has been decided. The implications for a culture change must also be considered as the different ways of being church reflect underlying norms and values so time will have to be invested in adapting or changing these. Changing a strong church culture takes time, usually much longer than the span of the average church appointment, a factor that is often ignored when making these appointments thus creating discontinuity and putting real development at risk.

Time is the great leveller for we all have twenty-four hours a day. It can be used wisely or well, for it is our most precious resource, more important than money, although in some ways similar to the word money in our language games as we have seen. The Church needs to be responsive as well as reactive; responsive in the sense that it is trying to take people and point people to a better future, one with God, but reactive, too, in that it must be open to the needs and demands, often unexpected, that are made upon it. The reactive can drive out the responsive, but equally, the responsive and strategic part of leadership needs to be open to need as it arises. Getting the balance right is essential to good church leadership.

QUESTIONS

- How far is it helpful to compare time with money?
- What time does your church leadership spend in strategic planning for the future?
- Are the Dulles based models helpful in developing a church?
- How are volunteers managed?
- Which groups seem to get most of the leadership time? Are there people who get no time? If so, why?

Chapter 10

RESURRECTION LEADERSHIP

As was stated in the Foreword, some of the material for this book has been first used in leadership workshops in a variety of places. As part of these workshops a model for leadership was proposed for discussion and debate. We called it the resurrection model because it is based on the post-resurrection appearances of Jesus highlighted in the gospels. We found the resurrection model to be particularly useful for building the leadership attributes of the laity because it focuses on the disciples' reactions to Jesus' appearances in the post-resurrection period. However, the model is not just about discipleship. The particular experiences of resurrection recorded by the Gospel writers also form a series of interesting avenues of exploration in terms of leadership.

RESURRECTION DISCIPLESHIP AND LEADERSHIP

The period after the resurrection and before Pentecost marks a time when Jesus appeared to the disciples, partly to reinstate his friendship and authority among them and partly to give guidance on how his new risen life will impact upon humankind. The resurrection appearances are significant for church leadership today because the Gospel writers reveal a holistic agenda for the future through the activity and purposes of Jesus in his revelation of himself. In totality, they constitute a series of encounters where Christ gradually probes deeper into the components of community and redemption. The five appearances considered here are the encounters of Mary in the garden on the day of the resurrection, the walk along the road to Emmaus in the evening, the appearances to the disciples in the evening of the first day of the week, and a second, a week later with Thomas present, and

156

finally a breakfast on a sea shore. It should be noted though that what is offered here is not a biblical analysis, commentary or exposition of the texts. It is rather an amalgam of the reflections on our experience as leaders, mixed with some of the ideas, comments and musing of the participants of the workshops mentioned above. The discussions and debates have tended to explore creatively how the biblical texts might appear for the purposes of being a church leader or a leadership team today, rather than find an accurate interpretation. In a kind of wisdom-literature way they may appear more like a mind map of the text, more like Bible reading notes than an argued essay. What is also the case generically in what follows is that sometimes the model applies specifically to individual leaders and sometimes to a leadership team. Sometimes the model assumes more than one of the attributes outlined are possible in a single individual, but also that the totality of the model cannot be achieved in one man as it did in Jesus. The specific local constitution of church leadership will incorporate individual leaders acting collaboratively with other individuals, and teams acting collaboratively with other teams, just as the tambourine model envisaged.

Early morning in the garden (John 20.1-18)

The first appearance considered is the moment in the garden on Easter Sunday when Mary arrives at the tomb to attend to Jesus' body. We can imagine her, distressed and anxious, perhaps fearful and deeply shocked. Yet, practical tasks to do with burials have given her the courage to make the journey she never wanted to make. What goes through her mind and heart as she approaches the garden? And even more, when she sees the tomb laid open she may have asked what had happened – robbers, authorities, more trouble? The scene is obviously not what she expected for she runs for Peter and the 'disciple Jesus loved', and together they begin to run back towards the epicentre of the event.

John arrives quickly, but Peter enters first, and after their encounter with the empty tomb, Mary is left on her own weeping. As she stoops and looks in she sees the angels and speaks with them about wanting to find Jesus. At that moment Jesus appears. He appears to be an ordinary person whom she mistakes for the gardener. He asks her what she wants and she tells him, and then the *kairos* moment, the pivotal point of the encounter occurs. He speaks her name and instantly she recognizes him.

Was it his intonation, or his authority or his presence that reveals who he is? Whatever it was, she is changed in a moment and sees not another human being, but her Lord. Jesus goes on to confirm that all has changed, as he proclaims that his Father is now her Father and his God is her God too. This is a moment of profound reclaiming of Mary's being, and indeed all people who live in the light of the resurrection. We all have the possibility of this re-identification. Jesus, as Lord, is able in one moment, in a garden to name her, and in so doing, redeem her. If this has some echo of Eden, some significance in the reclaiming of a past relationship, then perhaps it is meant. The relationship of humankind and God in the garden is restored, and the first to realize it is a woman.

Church leadership is often about managing situations and caring for people. In both cases entering into a close relationship and taking responsibilities seriously are crucial factors to the success of the leader. Sometimes leaders endeavour to change situations without knowing what they are about, what they involve and often this ends in conflict or failure. The task of getting to know people and situations is vital to the success of care and the exercise of ministry. In order to do this a leader employs all their being. In a sense Jesus' use of the single word *Mary* sums this up. His voice demonstrates a deep knowledge of her situation and hope for the future.

What is it in leadership that is conveyed by the voice? The voice is such an intimate part of our being. Each voice is unique and personal. It is formed not only from the physiology of a person, but also from nurturing. How we sound often has as much to do with what we mean as the content of what we say. Church leadership involves using the voice in preaching, prayer, and pastoral work in an unusually significant way. Liturgically, leaders pronounce forgiveness, offer praise, proclaim commandments, encourage, warn and advise. Each demands different tones and timbres of the vocal range. And here Jesus manages, in one word, to change the rest of Mary's life by speaking her name.

Naming is part of the ontological process of creating identity, and also, in terms of the 'adamic' naming of the creation, it means sharing in the personal and pastoral responsibility for creation. In Mary's case, Jesus identifies her by speaking her name as she looks for him, and then he indicates his care as he alludes to his Father now being her Father also. If leaders are to exercise something of Jesus' resurrection ministry then they need to name people and tasks and take responsibility for them. Naming people, like when the names of the sick are read out in the intercessions does two things. It re-members the identity of the person and it distinguishes their boundary. The identity is essentially the essence of the person or situation made explicit. What it is that people and situations actually are, is illuminated, appreciated and owned. Naming means describing and recognizing a person or situation for what it is. But it also distinguishes who is who. It delineates boundaries – this situation, this place, this person, not that one – which in turn creates a sense of belonging-ness.

In the 'adamic' sense of naming, alongside belonging, lie duties of care. These will not be the same for everyone or every situation. Responsibilities are given, different in each individual case, to care for and protect. And alongside care is the ever-present imperative to stand out and stand up for the distinctiveness of being called a Christian. *Ecclesia* means called out and called to. This dual purpose of the Church's name creates a dynamic that is both centripetal and centrifugal. The centripetal magnetism is expressed through the bonds and links of care that hold the Church's cohesion. The centrifugal forces throw the Church from *cosiness* out towards an ever-enlarging universe and mission.

To follow Christ means to be named and continue to be named by him. After his baptism where the Father named him as the Son, he was exploded out into the wilderness to be tested. Yet in the temptation narrative he was not tested until he had spent much time with himself. Church leaders are named publically by the Church, which marks them out, and identifies the hallmarks on their lives. A church leader's task is to likewise call forth the Church in its identity, distinctness, gifting and mission. Newman's ecclesiology envisaged a church where the laity could and would exercise this naming in their leadership, not so much as individuals but en masse. Leadership, following this resurrection appearance, exercised either by the ordained or lay, will name people's vocations, name the ever renewing relationship we have with God and name situations that invite God's providence, pastoral responsibility and love.

EVENING ON THE EMMAUS ROAD (LUKE 24.13-35)

The appearance on the road to Emmaus is rich in depth and meaning. Two disciples are walking home from the epicentre of activity, Jerusalem. Jesus joins them and empathically listens and converses with them as they travel the journey. He explains to them from Scripture what has happened and why. When they get to the village, he makes to go on and they invite him to have supper with them. During the meal his identity is revealed when he breaks the bread, whereupon he disappears. They speak of what they thought and felt during the journey, and then set out back to Jerusalem to tell the others.

This is a beautiful and oft told story, lovely to read and muse on. But it also demonstrates something of the nature of Jesus' leadership and hence something for church leaders today. First is the fact that no matter why the disciples are walking away from Jerusalem and heading off home, Jesus still meets them. While the rest of the disciples are fearful but gathering together, these two are getting back to the safety of home. It is difficult to imagine just what the disciples felt when they saw Jesus arrested, flogged and then killed on the cross. It wouldn't be hard to imagine them thinking that part of their own selves had died also. They had invested heavily in his ministry, following him, identifying themselves with his message, even doing some things he had done. But now everything had changed. This had become very serious indeed. As they walk away Jesus meets them, not face to face but walking alongside. He listens empathically while they tell him of the events that had come about. His response is to try and help them make sense of it, to offer biblical reflection on their experience. What really makes them understand the significance of events and find freedom from their fears is his revelation of himself through the breaking of bread. In this, what suddenly dawns on them is the realization and recognition of the fact that he is alive. The example is clear. The leadership of the Church provides empathic consolation, and also the revelation of the personhood of Christ through the breaking of bread.

Leaders cannot be leaders unless they connect themselves to their people in some shape or form. Christ drew alongside. In all the appearances Jesus draws alongside, but in this one it is more explicit. The act of drawing alongside is not all that easy in churches. People's expectations of leaders are quite often to have someone up front. In the work I engage in with churches who are looking for a new leader they often say they want someone who will be a strong leader. Life can be easier that way – but not always grown-up. Jesus comes to the disciples as a fellow traveller, an equal, someone who asks questions. He asks them 'What are you discussing?' The Socratic method is not a bad one to adopt and individual leaders are often advised to do this in their first term with a new congregation. However, this wasn't in the first term. To go on asking questions and making people aware of their interpretations is a very powerful way of teaching. It involves close empathy mixed with good explanation, which of course in turn has implications for the continuing study and reflection on Scripture to be effective. After his explanations he comes to the house, is invited in and accepts the hospitality of a meal with them.

A sacrament makes known, through symbol, what is invisible, what is hidden within, what is beneficial about following God. The dominical sacrament of the Eucharist makes known the life, purpose and grace of Jesus and when we celebrate it, we follow the interesting shape of the actions Jesus performed at Emmaus. Gregory Dix writes about this in his seminal book, *The Shape of the Liturgy*,[1] and it is pertinent to both clergy and the laity. The metaphor, taking bread, blessing, breaking, and giving, is central to Christ's story. It features highly in the celebration of the Eucharist and it is also, by derivation, central to the story of all our lives. On the night before he died, Christ took bread, blessed, broke and gave it.[2] On the night after he was raised, he again took bread, blessed, broke and gave it.[3] It is a pre-passion and post-passion narrative. In this act, his followers remember him, and are re-membered into his body by the Spirit, for the sake of all humankind. churches re-enact the four-action pattern regularly in their liturgy. In its contemporary context this is a liturgical symbol of the commitment to the needs of the communities they serve. What does it mean for leaders of the Church?

Christ's ministry in the world today is an enactment of this four-fold action. Taking the bread, that is, receiving it into hands, encounters Christ in the palm of the hand. His hands were nailed to the cross, bound for humankind, but the bread that is placed in the palms of his followers is bread that frees the hands, and it summons the follower to place bread into other hands. This is where the leader and leadership team begin and sustain their work. The regularity of receiving this sustaining sacrament will vary, but its significance cannot be underestimated. All leaders and leadership teams are disciples at root, ministers in their gifting and called to serve others in their leadership of ministry.

Blessing the bread has elements of giving thanks for it, celebrating it. The relationship of the leader and team with Christ is one of mutual love, adoration and worship of God. The psalmist blesses the Lord, and becomes a blessing to the people. The responsive acts of worship

[1] Dix, G. (1945) *The Shape of the Liturgy*. London: D'Acre Press, pp. 48–102.
[2] Luke 22.19.
[3] Luke 24.30.

that God's people make, provoke God's blessing on people. Breaking the bread inevitably and understandably makes us think of something that is broken. In today's society some will throw out broken objects rather than mend them. Does this mean that it is the broken body of Christ that we give thanks for? There is a very powerful altar in St Michael's Church, Bath that is broken. The wood is cracked and the celebrant stands in front of a precarious table.[4] Yet the act of breaking can signify different things – breaking through, breaking open, breaking apart, breaking in, breaking up and breaking away can be painful, powerful and ultimately positive experiences. These phrases can reveal what Christ has done, is doing and may want to do in the world and individual lives. They are sometimes corrective, sometimes foundational, sometimes redirecting and always life-changing.

Given means that the bread is given away, shared, offered, let go of. It is not always easy to give things away. Leaders or leadership teams are people whose task is to enable and cope with this giving. Giving means loss, something is given away, yet it is a loss that yields gain to the giver. Earlier it was said that nothing is a given but always a gift. In a sense, the gift is caught up in the act of giving, like when a person gives the communion bread or wine to someone else. They give and share the gift that has been given by God. When Jesus gave the bread and wine, he gave himself to his followers. In one sense, he was proclaiming the coming of the Spirit who would become the Spirit of Christ in all believers. The Spirit's work is to make Christ known in the world and leaders are those who encourage and support the whole body to be bread and to give bread, give themselves and the bread of God to the hungry world.

Yet the Eucharistic sacramental act is not the only action of this event, for while the disciples were walking, another word was being broken open, Scripture. Christ used the opportunity to enable the disciples to see, from their Scriptures, that his death and rising were destined to happen. Similarly, some leaders are called to break open God's word. The four-fold shape can be applied just as much to the preaching of scripture as the bread in the Eucharist. The Scriptures are apprehended, taken into the possession of the preacher. They are appreciated, given thanks for, blessed with gratitude. They are broken open through a hermeneutic that reveals meaning and the message is presented, given, offered to all who wish to hear it. The

[4] See a reflection on brokenness by the Rector of St Michael's in Bath in Williams M. L. (2007) *Beauty and Brokenness*, London: SPCK.

preacher becomes a minister and leader of the process that lies at the heart of both word and sacrament. As the Scripture in the Emmaus road story is used to explain the event, it too gives the disciples faith – 'didn't our hearts burn!' The inspiration of Scripture reveals the background for what had happened and the prophetic history of the Messiah is enacted before them.

Leaders are called to interpret and to enable people find inter- pretation of the everyday events of their lives. Paula Gooder, in her book *Searching for Meaning* offers a panoply of interpretive techniques ranging from traditional criticisms to contemporary hermeneutics. The task of leaders who are called to preach or specifically handle God's word is not only to bring interpretation to scripture, but also to events in people's lives and make the connections. The need to put time aside and reflect on ministry and find an ordered way of doing some serious interpretive, reflective theology is crucial and yet sometimes difficult. As Richard Rohr puts it in *The Naked Now*: 'When so many become professional church workers without going through spiritual transformation at any deep level, religious work becomes a career, and church becomes something one attends.'[5] The opportunity given by the risen Christ is that leaders can observe, ask and listen, which might mean slowing down the pace, giving the kind of space a metaphorical walk home offers. He offers leaders his own self, and asks them to give this away. He provides the Spirit to set the Church on fire with love for him. When this happens then the results are truly transformative.

The Upper Room (John 20.19-23 and Luke 24.36-39)

The appearance of Jesus in the Upper Room on the evening of Easter day found the disciples gathered together in fear. Their association with Jesus, but more so, their utter fear of what happened on the final day of his life had led them to abandon him. Somehow they must have talked to one another and decided to gather in the Upper Room. Expecting the Roman authorities to pursue them, they met, fearful and yet strangely curious about these reported sightings. Leaders may not face such situations of impending or potential persecution too often in the West. This is not so for many in parts of the world which are hostile to other religions or Christianity. Even in the West, leaders

---

[5] Rohr, R. (2009) *The Naked Now*, New York: The Crossroad Publishing Company, p. 37.

will have to face and be with people who are fearful of life for reasons of economy, redundancy, violence, abuse and injustice, to name but a few. Jesus miraculously appears to the disciples and yet, according to Luke they do not recognize him, thinking him to be a ghost. He shows them his wounds, breathes on them and speaks the word *peace* before they recognize him.

The constant theme in these appearances is of hidden-ness leading to recognition. Christ offers them an extraordinary revelation of himself. Here it is his wounds that convince them as to who he is. On the road, or rather in the house in the village, it is the breaking of bread; in the garden it is his naming of Mary. In essence Jesus' resurrection authority is established by his revelation of himself as one who offers a new relationship with God, one who presides at the breaking of bread, and one who suffers and dies for others. This is further endorsed by the symbolic breathing on the disciples and the tongues of fire that appear on their heads. Peace is administered by breathing on them. New life is breathed into them and they experience a new sense of being alive. The fire sets them ablaze with the Gospel so that they no longer fear and peace replaces their anxiety. Yet they are also charged to go and bring or give peace to others. The two gifts of peace are for themselves and for others. Their hearts are healed of their deepest fears and they are sent out to become peacemakers.

Leaders are called to make themselves available to the opportunity of being changed. This can be difficult. A hubristic problem, one that involves excessive pride, occurs when the congregation puts a leader on a pedestal. In such circumstances, a church leader becomes open to over-control and in danger of acting in a patronizing way rather than as an equal adult. It becomes harder and harder to admit vulnerability or the need to change in various ways. Newman's phrase, 'to live is to change' is unwelcome when the cosiness of frequent strokes, in transactional analysis terms, have become the norm. For the disciples this was a moment of transformation, which in some ways they had to accept. There was little alternative. They had come to the end of the road with Jesus, the ball was in his court and they knew that no matter how much they had enjoyed his ministry and company on their journeys, he was now dead.

The imagery in the text is quite extraordinary. The use of a breath takes us to the heart of creation. The exhalation of Jesus' breath (who was supposedly dead), becomes an inhalation for the spiritually dead disciples, and they are made alive through his spirit, which in turn, becomes an exhalation of peace upon the world. The disciples are ordained with breath and fire to be peacemakers. They cannot do this until they have been freed from their anxieties and reinstated to their discipleship. They are impotent until Jesus' breath and fire brings them to life and sets them on fire.

The advent of widely spread spiritual direction or accompaniment for most leaders has begun to address the issues of remaining fresh and able to lead a congregation and community. It would be inconceivable for the disciples not to be talking about this experience for many months and years to come. Likewise it is essential for today's church leaders to learn from the opportunities spiritual direction and accompaniment offers. One disciple who probably spent more time talking to a spiritual director than many of the others was Thomas, because of his doubt and the way Christ dealt with it.

THOMAS, CHRIST AND THE DISCIPLES (JOHN 20.24-29)

Thomas clearly was not present at the first evening Upper Room experience, and he made his views plain during the week. As they gathered the next week, this time with Thomas, Jesus appeared and beckoned to him to touch his wounds and believe. Through the marks of suffering, Christ became known and he spoke about those who had not seen but believed. We are never told if Thomas did in fact put his hand into Christ's wounds. All we know is that Christ met him where he was.

The task of faith is to follow Christ, but how we do that is not always uniform. In fact it rarely follows a pattern. There have been those such as James Fowler who have tracked and identified stages of faith development, and their work has been regarded as helpful in general terms. In his book *Becoming Adult, Becoming Christian* he identifies six stages of faith development, intuitive-projective, mythic-literal, synthetic-conventional, individuative-reflective, conjunctive and universalizing faith. The first three are based on the life cycle. When we are babies we react intuitively, in early childhood story is important and we generally take the beliefs and values we learn in later childhood by convention into adolescence. In his fourth stage, as we begin our quest for interdependence, usually through independence, individuative concerns drive our belief enquiries. As we emerge into maturity we can see other perspectives and perhaps we seek some sort of conjunction between what we hold as faith and what others have discovered. The sixth stage, universalizing faith, is the lure to transforming relationships with others and transformation

across society. Fowler suggests that few are called to this degree of
faith.

In some senses Christ helps Thomas to move from a conventional
faith believed by all, to an individual one in which he takes the truth
on board for himself. Thomas is what we might call today an empir-
icist. He needs evidence and Jesus allows him to test his unbelief in
an action that will finally convince him, as an individual, that Jesus
is indeed alive. He is clearly sceptical about the opinions expressed
by the given convention of his fellow disciples during the week and
simply won't believe them. He wants factual evidence and a close up
encounter with Christ. Here I am – Did you really die? He does not
simply want to hear the good news, he wants to see it as well, and sight
is a different type of knowing than hearing. The event also speaks of
finding an empathy with Christ's sufferings. He is invited to place
his hand into the wound in his side and his fingers into the holes in
his hands and feet. This says something about the degree to which
leaders are called to share the sufferings of Christ. It is a reminder
that discipleship, ministry and the leadership of ministry is costly.
Yet, when he finds the truth, when he experiences it for himself, it
convinces him and he is prepared for anything. Some say he ministered in India, and if he did, then it is significant for the missionary
task that his conversion propelled him to the ends of the earth.

Church leaders and leadership teams lead their congregations from
the convention of faith to a deeper understanding and knowledge,
perhaps a reflective individuative faith, but certainly onward into an
ever deepening relationship with God. Included among the skills
needed to do this is listening for the slightly jarring voice of the
doubter who is wanting to hear the evidence for themselves. There
are of course those who will moan and doubt, who are not prepared
to see for themselves, but for those who articulate their need for
more than a general opinion, leaders need to lead them to facts
and reality. In fact they might be the next leaders in the Church.
Vocations to leadership come in many surprising forms. The voice
of individual enquiry can sometimes only be heard as disruptive or
out of line with the accepted wisdom or truth the Church holds.
However, a leader like the risen Christ will take note of the genuine
request of an enquirer to challenge, ask, wonder about and doubt
the conventional corpus of knowledge. When this happens then faith
can develop and doubt becomes no more than the vehicle by which
faith grows. Fowler's stages are useful but some find them even more
helpful when they are released from any kind of linear cumulative

effect, to become stages in a spiral or cycle. The enquirer can then return to the mythic stage and rediscover something from narratives, or find inspiration from other religions as the conjunctive stage offers.

Leadership in church cannot exist only with a didactic process of imparting faith statements. It needs to be able to work with doubt, story, external insights, intuition, norms and conventions, for these are the stuff of everyday life. As Fowler's book suggests in its title becoming adult is a vital part of becoming Christian, and not something that needs to be avoided. John Hull makes a similar point in *What Prevents Christian Adults from Learning*. Too often the Church has had a tendency to infantilize and avoided dealing with doubts. Mature leadership will recognize different ways of becoming faithful and exercising faith in everyday life.

THE SEASHORE (JOHN 21.1-19)

The final appearance occurred when the disciples were out fishing and saw Jesus (although, yet again they didn't recognize him) on the seashore. Jesus enabled them in their work to miraculously catch a number of fish. As they did, they once more recognized and remembered Jesus' ministry. Afterwards, they ate breakfast together on the seashore and Peter was instituted to new work – from fish to sheep. He is called to 'feed my sheep'.

There is a debate about the exact role Jesus played in this incident. Was he the miraculous director of the disciples in order that they were able to catch fish, or did he do what some would do as a regular occupation and stand a little higher up on a cliff and see where the fish were shoaling and direct the boat to them? The point here is not whether he performed a miracle, it is that he involved himself in the everyday work of the disciples. He was concerned about their livelihood and called them to a higher responsibility. He was not aloof in his resurrection body, indeed he went further and provided hospitality for them at the end of the working shift, sat with them and talked. In the midst of this he focused the task for Peter, reinstating him in so doing, by giving him a firm direction to feed sheep.

Relating theology and everyday life has been highlighted in earlier chapters. Here, Jesus makes the connection explicit. In the former appearances Jesus and his actions have an other-worldiness, whereas here the world of work and the calling to a vocation are inextricably linked. I will make you fishers of people. In one sense it must have

taken the disciples back to the times when they had been earning
their livings and life had a familiar routine. Jesus called them out
from their everyday jobs and called them together into his followers.
This changed their everyday life into lives that became part of a
wonderful adventure of discovery. After his death and resurrection
they returned to their work but Jesus entered their world once more
and offered them fellowship on the beach and enabled them to catch
the fish – more than they had imagined. In a reversal of the degra-
dation of work into toil in Genesis after the fall, toil is transformed
and becomes joyful work again. For all of them this was momentous
but for Peter this was a vocational moment. The one who had
betrayed Jesus is given his trust and charged to feed my lambs, take
care of my sheep, and feed my sheep.

Leaders and leadership teams have to be connected to those whom
they lead. It is not good for a leader to be disconnected, however the
connections they make can be different. Leadership can be exercised
in a directive way – cast your nets over there. It can be exercised in a
relational way – come, share breakfast with me. It can be exercised in
a commissioning or ordaining way – feed my sheep. Leadership can
also be exercised from behind, in, among, or in front of people. In
a sense Jesus was behind the disciples when both he and them were
looking to catch the fish. Jesus could see where they were and they
couldn't. He led them to the catch. It can be exercised from among
people as when he sat among them eating the fish. It can also be an
in front of people as when he confronts Peter to 'feed my sheep' yet
he concludes by saying follow me.

The training teams of the Anglican dioceses of Bath and Wells, and
Bristol carried out some relatively informal research to ascertain what
makes teams and leaders work together best. Approximately thirty
parishes and benefices were asked face-to-face questions and filled
in questionnaires. After the results were analyzed and considered
it became apparent that the churches that worked best together
were those who put relationships first, the discovery of people's
gifts next and the bringing together of vision third. Out of the good
relationships gifts emerged and from that a vision for the Church
was discovered. In one sense this wasn't rocket science, yet it has to
be taken seriously that when leaders come alongside their people,
take time to enjoy and cultivate a friendship, then the people are
confident to reveal what God might be saying in terms of their
vocation and the leader can then discern what this might mean for
the individual and church. A vision for the Church begins to become

obvious as the Spirit leads individuals and groups. The task of the leaders or leadership team is to discern this and name it.

SUMMARY

This has been the beginning of some musings on these incidents. It doesn't include the Ascension, which could form a sixth appearance and of course it cannot take into account the many appearances that we are told happened but not with any detail. It has emerged from those who have come together to examine the leadership of Jesus at this moment in his ministry, and is the background information that is used to look at some leadership issues with current leaders by the authors. It has also begun to form some material for use with churches going through a change of leader, for it correlates precisely in time with the exiting of a leader and the anticipation of a new situation.

In the garden Mary is called by name and given a new relationship with God, a closer and more intimate relationship. The two disciples on the Emmaus road discover through Word and sacrament how to interpret the signs of the times. The disciples in the Upper Room are *ordained* by Jesus with breath and fire to become peacemakers. Thomas finds that his doubts lead to faith and his unbelief is transformed by a deep encounter with Christ. The disciples on the seashore, dismayed by their unsuccessful work are charged with a new vocation and Peter *ordained to* a pastoral and missionary task. Leaders and leadership teams are given the responsibility to enable these things and more.

The resurrection leadership model is an example of the possibilities of leadership training that embraces theological principles at its core. It reminds leaders that everyone is by default a disciple before they are a leader and the exercise of ministry is an essential foundation to the task of a leader. It also suggests that there is a dimension beyond human capacity needed when involved in church leadership. The risen Christ, through the Holy Spirit is active in ministry and witness and the emphasis on the Gospel needs to include the post-resurrection life of Christ as well as his ministry on earth before and during his passion. Resurrection leadership means learning how to enable congregations come to terms with their status and situation in the light of the resurrection, to name it and see it transformed by Christ's power; to identify where God is particularly working in, around and beyond the communities of the Church.

Within this there is a vital interpretative exercise to explore the possibilities that God may wish to pursue. Discerning and equipping the congregation means asking the Holy Spirit to breath life into people, giving them the fire of the Spirit to effect transformation. There will be times when, like Jesus on the seashore, individuals will need encouragement and even reinstatement to focus and direct their ministries. The model forms the basis of a discussion as to how these principles might become part of the transformative process of the Church within its own walls and, more importantly, in the communities it serves.

CONCLUSION

Towards the end of the last century many people were asking whether the churches could be revived after the steep decline in churchgoing that occurred in the 1960s which still continues today. The causes of this are complex but it has left modern Britain with a moral and spiritual vacuum in a context in which powerful voices express hostility to faith and particularly to the Christian faith. The problems that our society faces whether they are economic, social, and political or moral do not, it seems, make people turn in larger numbers to the churches. Is this because these churches are not confident enough of the Christian message nor offer real accessible guidance and fellowship? Are some too confident in their fundamentalist lack of concern for real questions that are difficult to answer?

To be a person of faith is, in an important sense, to be counter-cultural otherwise what place would there be for conversion, repentance, holiness or prophecy? We have argued that one of the key images of the Church today should be, following the Gospels, 'leaven' or 'salt'; in other words the Church is a community which is concerned with real change from within society itself. It does not exist simply to be the religious arm of the state or to provide rites of passage. In John Wesley's memorable phrase it exists to 'comfort the afflicted and afflict the comfortable'. Christianity is a religion of healing but also of challenge to view life and the world differently. Yet there is evidence of a deep-seated spiritual concern expressed in commitment to causes or to forms of spiritual exploration that go far beyond organized religion. Has organized religion got in the way of real spirituality?

One of the most challenging books about mission was written by Vincent Donovan, a Catholic missionary to the Masai in 1978. He became convinced that the existing missionary structures of his church seemed to have had no effect on bringing people to the Gospel. He went to the Masai simply to reach out to them and to talk with them where they were without the organizational trappings that

171

seemed to have encased the Gospel and prevented it being heard. When he approached them, and explained that what he wanted to do was to talk with them about God and the message of Christianity, he was greeted by the comment 'If that is why you came here, why did you wait so long to tell us about this?'[1] He realized that the task was not so much about revival but about re-founding the Church by going to a place where none of us has been before.

Two things must come together, he says, 'the gospel and the sacred arena of people's lives':

> The result, I think, could be a new church in a new place, a new ministry of the priesthood of all believers, away from the temple, far from the altar and sanctuary, out in the midst of human life as it is lived in the neighbourhoods, in the teeming, forlorn city; a ministry of politics and law, a ministry of commerce, a ministry of sports and entertainment and music, a ministry of human life and love; a ministry in which all of life and all of the world would be offered up with the bread and wine. All this is my body.[2]

Some may argue that Europe is not Africa in that Europe has heard the Gospel and to a large extent seems to have rejected it, whereas in other parts of the world, it is something fresh. Nevertheless Donovan's insight has relevance in that we may allow the increasingly bureaucratic nature, centralism and institutionalism of the Church to get in the way of what it should really be. Institutions are very greedy: they feed on people's time and energies and continually demand more of the same simply to perpetuate themselves. Moreover, they have a tendency to become more and more like secular bodies in their structures, procedures, values, outlook and ways of acting. Churches need to be institutional in order to act fairly and efficiently but they are much more than institutions and their ordained leaders especially should not be reduced to fulfilling a merely functional institutional role, taking their perspectives from the society around them. This is why we have emphasized the importance of ecclesiology, the theology of vocation and sacrificial giving. To be ordained is much more than a job although some contemporary language seems to make it sound exactly like that. An efficient bureaucratic organization is not necessarily a very spiritual or missionary one or a community where real fellowship can be found. Having said that, a church that ignores proper institutional requirements may become a very unjust body.

---

[1] Donovan, V. (1982) *Christianity Rediscovered* (2nd edn). London: SCM Press, p. 22.

[2] Ibid. p. vii.

Our attempt to bring together the two languages of theology and organizational theory is in order to strike a balance and to remind us not only of what ultimately the Church is which requires the language of metaphor to describe it, but also to be run well.

Donovan's story reminds us of the importance of leadership being imaginative, of the need to take risks and of the necessity of the Church being able to adapt to new challenges while being faithful to the past. Fidelity to the past is not the same as replication of it but rather of being faithful to the Gospel roots which give us life. We have argued that the particular role of ecclesiologically symbolic leadership is to hold up the vision to the people who can then be led to new places, like the People of Israel under Moses. The Church is fundamentally in a covenant relationship with the God who travels with it to incarnate the Gospel anew for every age. If God is our fellow-traveller, then we also need to travel together ourselves. The New Testament message is fundamentally one of working together using the gifts and charisms of all for the sake of the Kingdom. The emasculation of the laity that has been so much part of the history of Christianity impoverishes and disables the Church. The laity needs to be enabled, not only to perform their appropriate leadership and ministry within the Church but more importantly, to exercise their leadership and ministry within the world resourced by the Church. The ordained therefore need to see themselves as trustees of the vision, teachers, pastors, enablers of mission and fellow-disciples under the Gospel, not as do-it-all ministers stretched to breaking point.

This requires the Church to be a community of good relation-ships, of trust and co-responsibility for its work and mission. The 'tambourine' model put forward in this book only works on that basis. Arguably, the role of the ordained person becomes more, not less important, since it is the test of leadership to bring about a mature, adult, trusting ethos and to 'hold the ring'. The 'pyramid' model of church negates that position, depending largely on authority, one-way communication and legislative enactments. It prevents the ordained leader from really being a leader, positioning him or herself strategically for the good of the whole. The ethos that supports this will not happen overnight for it requires the community to be a learning church also, exploring what the Gospel means in this place and in this time. Leaders, whether clerical or lay, need to be people of vision and of courage but also of humility as inevitably mistakes will be made in the search for ways forward. A trusting community is able to forgive and use these occasions as ones from which they can learn. A good leader will model this.

How can such leaders be formed? Much thought has been given to this in recent years but the kind of qualities being emphasized in this book are not easily susceptible to measurement or 'benchmarks' although these may have their place as 'competencies'. What is required is good character formation also and that can normally only be done within some kind of community experience where spirituality and wisdom is imbibed as well as knowledge and skills acquired. Leaders need to be people of human and spiritual depth and this requires time for otherwise leadership formation will simply be about the acquisition of basic competencies and little else.

What the Church can learn from some notable examples in the business world is the importance of clarity of purpose, of values being communicated and incarnated at every level and of giving a service of value in which it takes pride. Very often such businesses have a real sense of partnership among the staff and thus a sense of common ownership in what the firm does and stands for. Each has their part to play. While the Church is not a profit-making organization, it has much to learn from these examples of organizations where people really matter in a way that lifts their willingness to contribute the skills and talents and make a difference.

The very uncertain and troubled world in which today's Christians find themselves, needs leaders of wisdom whether they be politicians, industrialists, financiers, educationalists or any other position of power and influence. If the Church is to renew itself, then, leaders of wisdom able to bring their influence to bear upon the human stage for the good of the whole. If the rising interest in spirituality is a symptom of the individual's search for wisdom or a cause to live by as an alternative to the values we find around us, so society often looks to new leaders with an almost messianic hope to lead us in a different direction. The crises of the late twentieth and early twenty-first centuries reveal deep flaws in the world humans have created. At the same time, faith has become privatized and the Church, riven by its own internal dissensions and difficulties, is seemingly unable to speak and be heard.

In our earlier chapters, we spoke of the Augustinian option, of being prepared to be a people of hope without much external evidence of a successful outcome, the other options being simply to throw in the towel or to retreat into some kind of safe enclave. These other options were not Jesus' way even as he journeyed towards

Jerusalem for the last time. The Gospel is about the redeemability of all things and to that all Christians are called to play their part.

At the end of his visit to the UK in September 2010, Pope Benedict XVI at Westminster Hall on 17 September outlined a further task for Christian leaders in a society which had elements of aggressive atheism within it. He spoke of the marginalization of Christianity that he detected in society 'even in nations which place great emphasis on tolerance'. On the contrary there is a need for religion to be seen as 'a vital contributor to the national conversation'. He reminded his hearers of the 'legitimate role of religion in the public square' and the need to 'seek ways of promoting and encouraging dialogue between faith and reason at every level' for the 'good of our civilization'.[3]

In this book we have argued for a *conspiratio* or 'breathing together' of clergy and laity and the development of leadership of varying kinds. Both groups within the Church have their part to play in this dialogue with society and need to be equipped to do this. For this, education in the Christian faith is vital as is the kind of ethos that promotes learning together, listening and empathy which are the essentials that underpin all dialogue. Perhaps the Church of the twenty-first century needs to discover once again how to look outwards in faith rather than be preoccupied with internal differences and arguments and to prepare itself for the long haul of St Augustine. 'In the world but not of it' is an uncomfortable place to be and demands particular skills of leadership, maintaining hope in uncertain times, but in the end it is the only place to be in fidelity to the Gospel:

> Keep thou my feet; I do not ask to see
> The distant scene; one step enough for me.[4]

[3] http://www.vatican.va_/phome_en.htm
[4] J. H. Newman Lead Kindly Light.

APPENDIX – MODELS OF THE CHURCH (ADAPTED FROM DULLES MODELS OF THE CHURCH)

Image	1. Institution	2. Mystical Communion	3. People of God (variant)	4. Sacrament	5. Herald	6. Servant	7. Disciple
Keywords	• Teaching • Sanctifying • Governing • Hierarchy • Pastoral Authority • Jurisdiction • Office • Visible organizational unity	• Spiritual • Body of Christ • Interpersonal • Community • Divine origin • Imperfect realization of Kingdom • Spirit-filled and led • Divinization • Mystery • Liturgy	A variation of Mystical Communion model with some differences: • Christ as leader • Pilgrim people on journey • No abiding city • Provisional body • Future looking • Seeking	• Community of encounter with Christ • Worshipping community: Eucharistic • Church as symbol as well as sign to others • Liturgy as celebration • Means of grace • Gifted by Spirit • Church as leaven	• Word of God • Proclamation • Mission • Eschatology • Conversion • Faith • Authority of Scripture • Community of believers • Response	• *Diakonia* • Service • Dialogue with others • Christ for others • Suffering servant • Hope to world • Option for the poor • Servant authority	• Cost and risk of discipleship • Leave all for Christ • Christ as teacher and model • Father as teacher • Variety of gifts and vocations • Spirit as guide • Church as teacher and as disciple • Catechumen • Faith commitment

Advantage	• Endorsed by historical Church documents • Clarity about membership and goals • Structures claimed as based on Revelation • Continuity and stability • Corporate identify • Institutional loyalty	• Personal • Biblical basis especially in John and Ephesians • Mystery in worship • Corporate communion with God • Role of Spirit • Gifts of Spirit • Supernatural emphasis	• Emphasizes Christian journey led by God • OT basis especially Exodus • Open to change • Unmaterialistic • Emphasis on fellowship • Ecumenical • Well supported by Tradition • Subordinates institutional • Less prone to over-divinization of Church	• Social and visible sign of grace • Spiritual unity • Eucharistic emphasis • Unites best of models 1 and 2 • Grace working beyond limits of visible Church • Inspires loyalty but allows for Church as human • Biblical basis especially in Institution Narratives in Gospels and Paul	• Puts response and witness of faith to the fore • Church as proclaimer of Gospel • Biblical basis especially in Synoptic Gospels • Mission-centred • Active commitment emphasized	• Not authoritarian • Takes world seriously and all sources of truth • Strong sense of service to world • Christ as servant role model • Biblical basis especially in Gospels and Acts	• Emphasis on Christ as our master avoids any undue elevation of human authority • Stresses cost of discipleship and how the Church should live • Biblical basis especially in Synoptic Gospels • Stresses separateness and demands of Christian life • Church as contrast society

Disadvantage						
• Meagre basis in Scripture or Early Church • Clericalism • Exaggerates need for authority • Minimizes prophetic • Tends to discourage creative and fruitful theology • Unattractive to an age viewing organizations as self-serving/repressive	• Tendency to divinize church too much • Obscures relationship of visible and invisible elements of Church • Lack of clarity about members' sense of identity and mission • Too much emphasis on interiority?	• Mostly OT-based • Some tension between this and Mystical Communion: ambiguity about 'communion' • Tension between image and reality • Not enough emphasis on Christ and worship	• Tendency to narrow sacramentalism • Insufficient emphasis on Word and Proclamation • Tends to under emphasize mission • Not so ecumenically attractive	• More congregational view of Church rather than worldwide body • Tendency to overemphasize written and spoken word at expense of other forms of Gospel presence • May ignore context • Tendency to one way communication • Tendency to underplay importance of spiritual life	• May avoid prophetic challenge and proclamation when needed • Tendency to secularization • Mission as service only • Lack of mystical sense • Confusion of suffering servant concept with service to world at expense of the Gospel and worship	• Says little about worship • May set community too much apart from the world • Excessive demands on people with busy lives • Church may be seen simply as an association of free volunteers • Tendency to individualism

QUESTIONS

1. What is the predominant model in the church(es) for which you have responsibility or in which you are a leader?

2. Is the predominant model appropriate? If not, to what model might your church/congregation be aspiring to in the light of its contemporary context?

3. What practical steps would you take to develop each of the models and void or minimize the disadvantages?

4. What kinds of leadership and ministers will be required to realize any of the models?

BIBLIOGRAPHY

All quotations of Newman's works used in this thesis, unless specified in the footnotes, are from the uniform edition now available at: http://www.newmanreader.org.

The abbreviations used are as below. The dates in brackets pertain to the original publication date followed by the later date when the text was reprinted by Newman in the Longman uniform edition.

Apol.	Apologia pro Vita Sua {1864, 1873)
Ari.	The Arians of the Fourth Century {1833,1871}
Dev.	An Essay on the Development of Christian Doctrine {1845, 1878}
Hist. II	Historical Sketches, Volume II {Various, 1872}
Hist. III	Historical Sketches, Volume III {Various, 1872}
Idea	The Idea of a University defined and illustrated {1852 and 1858,1873}
OCF	On Consulting the Faithful in Matters of Doctrine {1859, 1871} (ed.) John Coulson, (London: Chapman, 1961)
Prepos.	Lectures on the Present Position of Catholics in England {1851, 1872}

Abbott, W. M. (General ed.) (1966) *The Documents of Vatican II.* London: Geoffrey Chapman.

Adair, J. (1983) *Effective Leadership.* London: Pan Macmillan

Apostola, N. (ed.) (1998) *A Letter from Christ to the World.* Geneva: WCC Publications.

The Apostolate of the Laity <http://www.vatican.va/archive/ hist_councils/ii_vatican_council/documents/vat-ii_decree_ 19651118_apostolicam-actuositatem_en.html>.

The Archbishop's Council (2003) *Formation for Ministry Within a Learning Church,* London, Church House Publishing.

The Archbishop's Council (2007) *The Mission and Ministry of the Whole Church: Biblical, Theological and Contemporary Perspectives,*

GS misc. 854. London: The General Synod of the Church of England.

Astley, J. (2002) *Ordinary Theology*. Aldershot: Ashgate Publishing.

Astley, J. et al. (2004) *The Idea of a Christian University*. Milton Keynes: Paternoster.

Avis, P. (1992) *Authority, Leadership and Conflict in the Church*. London: Mowbray.

Avis, P. (2002) *Anglicanism and the Christian Church* (revised and expanded edn). London: Continuum.

Avis, P. (2003) *A Church Drawing Near*. London: T&T Clark.

Avis, P. (2005) *A Ministry Shaped by Mission*. London: T&T Clark.

Avis, P. (ed.) (2002) *The Christian Church: An Introduction to the Major Traditions*. London: SPCK.

Barrow, S. & Smith, G. (2001) *Christian Mission in Western Society*. London: Churches Together in Britain.

Beattie, T. (2007) *The New Atheists*. London: Darton, Longman & Todd.

Bonhoeffer, D. (1963) [1930] *Sanctorum Communio: A Dogmatic Enquiry into the Sociology of the Church*, trans. by R. Gregor Smith. London: Collins.

Bosch, D. J. (1980) *Witness to the World*. London: Marshall, Morgan and Scott.

Bosch, D. J. (1991) *Transforming Mission: Paradigm Shifts in Theology of Mission*. New York: Orbis.

Bruce, S. (2002) *God is Dead, Secularization in the West*. Oxford: Blackwell.

Butler, B. C. (1962) *The Idea of the Church*. London: Darton, Longman & Todd.

Carter, C. A. (2006) *Rethinking Christ and Culture*. Grand Rapids: Brazos Press.

The Catholic Bishops Conference of England and Wales (1995) *The Sign we Give : Report from the Working Party on Collaborative Ministry*. Chelmsford: Matthew James Publishing.

Chadwick, O. (1957) *From Bossuet to Newman*. Cambridge: Cambridge University Press.

Chadwick, O. (1991) *Michael Ramsey: A Life*. Oxford: Oxford University Press.

The Children's Society (2009) *A Good Childhood: Searching for Values in a Competitive Age*. London: Penguin.

Christifideles laici http://www.vatican.va/holy_father/john_paul_ii/apost_exhortations/documents/hf_jp-ii_exh_30121988_christifideles-laici_en.html.

Church House Publishing, (1995) *A Time for Sharing – Collaborative Ministry in Mission,* Board of Mission Occasional Paper No. 6. London: Church House Publishing.

Congar, Y. (1957) *Lay People in the Church,* trans. By Donald Attwater. London: Bloomsbury Publishing.

Congar, Y. (1999) *I Believe in the Holy Spirit,* trans. by David Smith. New York: The Crossroad Publishing Company.

Coulson, John (1970) *Newman and the Common Tradition.* Oxford: Clarendon Press.

Coulson, John (1981) *Imagination and Belief.* Oxford: Clarendon Press.

Craig, Y. (1996) *Tomorrow is Another Country,* GS misc. 467. London: Church House Press.

Culler, A. D. (1955) *The Imperial Intellect: A Study of Newman's Educational Ideal.* London: Oxford University Press.

D'Costa, G. (2005) *Theology in the Public Square.* Oxford: Blackwell Publishing. Farley, E. (1994) *Theologia: The Fragmentation and Unity of Theological Education.* Philadelphia: Fortress Press.

Daniélou, J. (1996) *Prayer: The Mission of the Church,* trans. by D. L. Schindler. Edinburgh: T&T Clark.

Davie, Grace (2002) *Europe: The Exceptional Case, Parameters of Faith in the Modern World.* London: Darton, Longman & Todd.

Dawkins, R. (2006) *The God Delusion.* London: Bantam Press.

Dix, G. (1945) *The Shape of the Liturgy.* London: D'acre Press.

Donovan, V. (1982) *Christianity Rediscovered* (2nd edn). London: SCM Press.

Dulles, A. (1974, 1987) *Models of the Church* (2nd edn). Edinburgh: T & T Clark.

Dulles, A. (2002) *Models of the Church* (ext. edn). New York: Doubleday.

Edwards, D. L. (1994) *What is Catholicism?* London: Mowbray.

Farmer, D. H. (ed.) (1965) *The Life of Cuthbert in The Age of Bede,* trans. by J. F. Webb. London: Penguin Books.

Femiano, S. D. (1967) *Infallibility of the Laity: The Legacy of Newman.* New York: Herder & Herder.

Flannery, A. (ed.) (1996) *Vatican Council II: The Conciliar and Post Conciliar Documents* (revised edn, Vol. 1). New York: Costello Publishing.

Francis, L. & Thatcher, A. (eds) (1990) *Christian Perspectives for Education.* Leominster: Gracewing.

Freire, P. (1972) *Pedagogy of the Oppressed,* trans. by Myra Bergman Ramos. Harmondsworth: Penguin Books.

General Synod of the Church of England (1985) *Faith in the City – A Call for Action by Church and Nation.* London: Church House Publishing.

George, T. (ed.) (1990) *John Calvin and the Church.* Louisville: Westminster/John Knox Press.

Gill, R. (ed.) (1996) *Theology and Sociology: A Reader.* London: Cassell.

Goheen, M. W. (July 2002) 'As the Father has sent me, so I am sending you: Lesslie Newbigin's missionary ecclesiology' in *The International Review of Mission* Vol. 91, No. 362. Geneva: WCC Publications.

Gooder, P. (2008) *Searching for Meaning: An Introduction to Interpreting the New Testament.* London: SPCK.

Greenwood, R. (1994) *Transforming Priesthood.* London: SPCK.

Guitton, J. (1964) *The Church and the Laity: From Newman to Vatican II,* trans. by Malachy Gerard Carroll. New York: Alba House.

Hahn, C. A. (1985) *Lay Voices in an Open Church.* New York: The Alban Institute.

Handy, C. (1985) *Gods of Management.* London: Souvenir Press

Handy, C. (1989) *The Age of Unreason.* London: Business Books.

Hanson, A. T. & Hanson, R. P. C, (1987) *The Identity of the Church.* London: SCM Press.

Hastings, A. (1986, 1991), *A History of English Christianity 1920–2000* (3rd and 4th edn). London: SCM Press.

Hill, E. (1988) *Ministry and Authority in the Catholic Church.* London: Chapman.

Hull, J. M. (1985) *What Prevents Christian Adults from Learning.* London: SCM Press Ltd.

Hutton, W. (1996) *The State We're In* (new and revised edition). London: Vintage.

Jarvis, P. and Walters, N. (eds) (1993) *Adult Education and Theological Interpretations.* Malabar: Krieger Publishing,

Jay, A. (1967) *Management and Machiavelli.* London: Hodder.

Kellermann, B. W. (ed.) (1994) *A Keeper of the Word: Selected Writings of William Stringfellow.* Grand Rapids: Eerdmans.

Kerkhofs, J. (1995) (ed.) *Europe Without Priests?* London: SCM.

Kerr, F. (2007) *Twentieth Century Catholic Theologians.* Oxford: Blackwell.

Kinast, R. L. (2000) *What Are They Saying About Theological Reflection?* New York: Paulist Press.

Küng, H. (1968) *The Church.* London: Search Press.

Lakeland, P. (2004) [2002] *The Liberation of the Laity: In Search of an Accountable Church.* London: Continuum.

Lumen Gentium <http://www.vatican.va/archive/hist_councils/ii_vatican_council/documents/vat-ii_const_19641121_lumen-gentium_en.html>.

Macquarrie, J. (1972) *The Faith of the People of God: A Lay Theology.* London: SCM Press.

Macquarrie, J. (1997) *A Guide to the Sacraments.* London: SCM Press.

McCann, J. F. (1993) *Church and Organisation: A Sociological and Theological Enquiry.* London: Associated University Press.

McFague, S. (1983) *Metaphorical Theology.* London: SCM Press.

Melinsky, M. A. H. (1992) *The Shape of the Ministry.* Norwich: The Canterbury Press.

Merrigan, T. (1991) *Clear Heads and Holy Hearts: The Religious and Theological Ideal of John Henry Newman.* Louvain: Peeters Press.

The Methodist Church, Faith and Order Committee (1995) *Called to Love and Praise: Report to Conference.* Peterbrough: Methodist Publishing House.

Milbank, J. (1990) *Theology & Social Theory.* Oxford: Blackwell.

Milbank, J. (2003) *Being Reconciled: Ontology and Pardon.* London: Routledge.

Minear, P. S. (1961) *Images of the Church in the New Testament.* London: Lutterworth Press.

Moltmann, J. (1977) *The Church in the Power of the Spirit,* trans. by Margaret Kohl. London: SCM Press.

Nazir-Ali, M. (2001) *Shapes of the Church to Come.* Eastbourne: Kingsway Publications.

Newbigin, L. (1995) *The Open Secret.* London: SPCK.

Newman, J. H. (1843) *Sermons on the subjects of the Day* (standard edition). London: Longman, Green & Co.

Newman, J. H. (1845) *An Essay on the Development of Christian Doctrine* (standard edition). London: Longman.

Newman, J. H. (1872–73) [2001] *Rise and Progress of Universities and Benedictine Essays.* Leominster: Gracewing.

Newman, J. H. (1893) *Meditations and Devotions* (2nd edn). London: Longman.

Niebuhr, H. Richard, (1952) *Christ and Culture.* London: Faber and Faber.

O'Connell Killen, P. and de Beer, J. (1994) *The Art of Theological Reflection.* New York: Crossroad Publishing Company.

Papesh, M. L. (2004) *Clerical Culture: Contradiction and Transformation.* Collegeville: Liturgical Press.

Pattison, S. (1997) *The Faith of the Managers: When Management Becomes Religion*. London: Cassell.

Percy, M. (2005) *Engaging with Contemporary Culture*. Aldershot: Ashgate Publishing.

Preston, G. (1997) *Faces of the Church*. Edinburgh: T&T Clark.

Quoist, M. et al. (1963) *Prayers of Life* (English translation). London: Gill and Macmillan.

Raiser, K. (1991) *Ecumenism in Transition* trans. by Tony Coates. Geneva: WCC Publications.

Rendle, G. R. (1998) *Leading Change in the Congregation*. Washington DC: The Alban Institute Publishing.

Rice, A. K. (1963) *The Enterprise and its Environment*. London: Tavistock.

Richards, M. (1995) *A People of Priests*. London: Darton, Longman & Todd.

Rohr, R. (2009) *The Naked Now*. New York: The Crossroad Publishing Company.

Sacks, J. http://www.bc.edu/research/cjl/meta-elements/texts/cjrelations/news/Sacks_Lambeth_Address.htm.

Sacks, Jonathan, '*Morals: the one thing markets don't make*', Opinion *The Times*, Saturday 21 March 2009.

Satir, V. (1972) *People-making*. California: Science and Behavior Books Inc.

Schillebeeckx, E. (1996) *Church: The Human Story of God*, trans. by John Bowden. New York: Crossroad Publishing.

Selznick, P. (1966) *Leadership in Administration: A Sociological Interpretation*. New York: Harper.

Suenens, L. (1968), *Co-responsibility in the Church*, London: Burns and Oates.

Sykes, S. (2006) *Power and Christian Theology*. London: Continuum International Publishing.

Sykes, S. et al. eds (1998 [1988]) *The Study of Anglicanism* (revised edn). London: SPCK.

Taylor, C. (2007) *A Secular Age*. Cambridge Mass: Belknap Press.

Tijmes L. A. & P. (eds) (1966) *The Church Inside Out*, trans. by W. L. Jenkins. London: SCM Press.

Van der Water, D. P. (April 2005) 'Transforming theological education and ministerial formation', *The International Review of Mission*, Vol. 94, No. 373, Geneva: WCC Publications.

Volf, M. (1998) *After Our Likeness*. Cambridge: William B. Eerdmanns Publishing Company.

Vorgrimler, H. (ed.) (1969) *Commentary On the Documents of Vatican II*, trans. by W. Glen-depel, and others. London: Burns and Oates.

Williams, M. L. (2007) *Beauty and Brokeness*. London: SPCK.

Williams, R. (2000) *Lost Icons*. London: T&T Clark.

Williams, R. (2004) *Anglican Identities*. London: Darton, Longman & Todd.

Wilson, B. R. (1982) *Religion in Sociological Perspective*. Oxford: Oxford University Press.

Wingate, A. (April 2005) 'Overview of the history of the debate about theological education' in *The International Review of Mission*, Vol. 94, No. 373. Geneva: WCC Publications.

Zizioulas, J. D. (1985) *Being As Communion*. London: Darton, Longman & Todd.

INDEX